Ally Sloper's Cavalry

Ally Sloper's Cavalry

From Mons to Loos with the Army Service
Corps During the First World War

Herbert A. Stewart

LEONAUR

Ally Sloper's Cavalry
From Mons to Loos with the Army Service Corps During the First World War
by Herbert A. Stewart

First published under the title
From Mons to Loos

Leonaur is an imprint
of Oakpast Ltd

ISBN: 978-1-78282-477-0(hardcover)
ISBN: 978-1-78282-478-7 (softcover)

http://www.leonaur.com

Publisher's Notes

The views expressed in this book are not necessarily
those of the publisher.

Contents

TYPES OF GERMAN
BEAUTY CAPTURED AT LODS

To
My
Mother

Preface

This little work does not profess to be a record of historical facts, but merely a series of impressions snap-shotted upon my mind as they occurred, and set down here in simple language; and if these snapshots can bring home to my readers some idea, however faint, of what war and its attendant miseries mean, then my labour will not have been in vain.

To those who may imagine that the British fighting man of today is not the equal of his forebears, who fought from Crécy and Agincourt to Albuera and Waterloo, I trust the story of Mons, the Aisne, Neuve Chapelle, and Ypres will set all doubts at rest.

For the enduring courage, remarkable cheerfulness under most depressing conditions, and marvellous patience of the Chapter xv. narrates the experience of my brother in the action fought at Hooge on the 9th August 1915 and following days.

As the term "Train" may perhaps be misunderstood by the reader, it would be as well to explain that this is the designation of a horse-transport unit consisting of baggage and food-supply waggons. The supply waggons after handing over their contents to the fighting troops proceed to refill, at the "Refilling Point" from the motor-lorries of the "Supply Column." This latter unit in its turn is refilled at railhead from the railway trains forwarded daily from the base.

CHAPTER 1

The Concentration in France

At 10 o'clock on the morning of the 11th August 1914, I passed through the dock gates at Southampton, and proceeding to the wharf discovered the vessel which was to carry me over to France. Incidentally, she was to convey about 1500 other khaki-clad sons of Britain, all bound on the same errand—to rid Belgium of the invader.

I had expected to see a *Dongola*, a *Plassy*, or at least a *Dilwara*, in the ship which was to convey me across the channel, and was therefore considerably disappointed when my gaze fell on the *Seven Seas*. This little vessel was a tramp steamer of about a thousand tons, snapped up by the Government which was glad to get anything that was available at the moment.

The usual bustle of departure was going on, steam derricks raising horses into the air supported in canvas slings under their bellies, then swinging them round over the quay and side of the ship to deposit them struggling on to the after-well deck. Other derricks forward were hoisting motorcars and packing them in the forewell. Troops were filing on board to deposit their rifles and accoutrements before returning to the quay to assist in the work of shipping stores. Pervading all was the usual smell of tarred rope and baled merchandise so obtrusive at all seaports.

By 4 o'clock the last horse and the last box of ammunition were stowed, the men filed on board, and the gangways were withdrawn. Then only did I notice that this sailing was unlike those others known to every soldierman when duty bound in peace time to the far corners of the earth. In those others are pictured a great troopship thronged with eager soldiers excited at the prospect of a voyage to "furrin parts"; many with their wives and families accompanying them, while on the quayside stand the cheering crowd who have come to say goodbye.

Who that has been an ocean voyage does not know the scene?

With us in the *Seven Seas*, (this vessel was torpedoed on 1st April 1915 by a German submarine off Beachy Head, and eleven of her crew were drowned), the picture was very different. There were no cheering crowds, all goodbyes had been said outside the dock gates, and the dingy little steamer, our crowded condition on her decks, and our very meagre field kits, brought home to us the great errand on which we were bound.

The troops on board were composed of half a battalion of the Middlesex Regiment, and detachments of Artillery, Engineers, and Army Service Corps, also some of the staff of the 3rd Division. Among the officers I met many old friends, some of whom I had last seen and served with years before in one of those far-flung outposts of Great Britain beyond the seas.

In some depression we watched the final preparations for departure, and in silence heard the clang of the engine-room bell and felt the first throbs of the engine.

As the warps were cast off and the vessel drew away from the quay, the embarkation staff and dock labourers raised a cheer to speed us on our way, and Thomas Atkins, who is never despondent for long, was soon "giving tongue" to "Tipperary."

While the steamer glided down Southampton Water the troops were called to "attention," and from the bridge the senior officer read out the king's farewell message to his soldiers. At its conclusion we cheered His Majesty, and the thunder of our voices rolled over the water, echoing back to us from the wooded shores.

By the time the vessel reached Calshot Castle the evening had fallen, one of those calm still evenings in summer when all seems peace and quietness. Not a ripple disturbed the surface of the sea, while behind the brown and green of the New Forest the sun slowly sank—a blaze of crimson.

The stillness of the evening laid its spell upon us, for a hush fell over the ship. Our eyes strayed over the water and rested on the distant hills of the Isle of Wight, while the simple manly words of the king's message filled our hearts.

Message from the King.

Buckingham Palace.

You are leaving home to fight for the safety and honour of my Empire. Belgium, whose country we are pledged to defend, has been attacked, and France is about to be invaded by the same powerful foe.

I have implicit confidence in you, my soldiers. Duty is your watchword, and I know your duty will be nobly done.

I shall follow your every movement with deepest interest, and mark with eager satisfaction your daily progress: indeed your welfare will never be absent from my thoughts.

I pray God to bless you and guard you and bring you back victorious.

George, R.I.

9th August 1914.

We thought of the dear ones we had left behind, and the great duty that awaited us ahead. Our task, we knew, must be full of peril. We knew, too, that many amongst us would never return.

Were we not about to pit our little army against a nation of soldiers—soldiers, too, who in the last half century had emerged gloriously triumphant from every war in which they had engaged—soldiers whose numbers are as the sands on the sea-shore, and whose discipline and military training are the envy and admiration of the world?

We knew that upon us Britons possibly depended the fate of Europe.

As I looked round on those tall lithe sons of old England, I felt that the king would not appeal in vain "to you my soldiers."

We Britons are a fighting race, which has matched its strength against all the nations of the world at some time or another, and have rarely had to acknowledge defeat.

At nightfall the vessel anchored off Ryde, and every one lay down on deck for a few hours' sleep. Those officers who were fortunate managed to secure a softer couch on the settees in the little saloon, or in one or two of the cabins kindly placed at our disposal by the ship's officers. It must be remembered that a tramp steamer of a thousand tons would not have accommodation for half the numbers placed on the little *Seven Seas*. However, the voyage was only a matter of a few hours, and the weather was fine and the sea calm.

At 1 a.m. on the 12th August the vessel proceeded on her voyage, dropping the pilot off Sandown and steering about S.S.E. for port "C." In mid-Channel we met a British destroyer, and it was a splendid sight watching her long lean hull racing through the bright sunlit sea, throwing the foam in fountains from her sharp bows, while from the stern fluttered "the flag that braved a thousand years the battle and the breeze." As she drew abreast of us her crew clustered on deck, waving their caps and cheering, while our troops crowded the side and swarmed up the rigging roaring their welcome across the sparkling water. With a friendly wave from her commander she drew ahead, and in a short time disappeared over the horizon. Her advent, however, gave us a feeling of security, and we felt that though the British Navy was out of sight yet our safety had been considered and provided for.

At 3 p.m. land was sighted ahead, and an hour later we passed between the pier-heads of Havre. The piers and quays and sandy-beach beyond were crowded with spectators watching our arrival, and great was the enthusiasm they displayed on catching sight of the khaki that thronged our decks. "*Vive l'Angleterre!*" "*Vivent les Anglais!*" greeted our ears on all sides, accompanied by much waving of hats and sticks and singing of the "*Marseillaise.*"

Our troops, as is common with Englishmen, were more amused than inspired by the demonstration ashore. Feeling, however, that some response was expected, they sang "Britannia" and "Tipperary," and even essayed the "*Marseillaise,*" whistling or humming the tune.

As soon as the vessel was berthed, the disembarkation of the troops, horses, and stores commenced. The various detachments were fallen in, in full marching order, facing the ship, and marched off to the rest camp.

Individual officers not on duty with troops proceeded to the base commandant's office, where they received their instructions as to how, when, and where to proceed to their destinations. I found myself with several others billeted at the Hotel Terminus for the night, with orders to proceed by train next day at noon to an unknown destination.

The base commandant's office was close to the docks, and at the berth of the Compagnie Transatlantique lay the giant liner *France*. I strolled on board with a friend, and found that the vessel had been waiting to proceed with her cargo and passengers for the last eight days, but was not permitted to commence her voyage to New York until the German cruisers on the high seas had been located, and it was considered safe for her to do so.

Seated in a comfortable armchair in the palatial lounge, sipping an iced lager, I watched with interest the cosmopolitan crowd of people who composed her passengers.

Later in the evening we sallied forth in search of dinner, and guided by Captain Réné Rumplemayer—a smart and most courteous officer of the French artillery attached to the British Army—sat down to an excellent meal in the best *café* in the town.

There were many other people in the restaurant seated in groups round small tables. French officers in bright-coloured uniforms, private soldiers in *cuirassier* and dragoon regiments, civilians with the corners of their napkins tucked into their ample waistcoats, and one or two women smartly though conspicuously dressed.

Among the diners pointed out to us was Prince Murat, dressed in the uniform of a *sous-officier* of dragoons. He was a tall, rather stout, heavy looking man, with regular features, full face, and fair complexion. He did not convey to one's mind any resemblance to that bold, ambitious, reckless adventurer who became King of Naples.

After an excellent night's rest and a bath, for which I was charged two *francs*, I collected my servant, horse and kit from the docks where they had spent the night, and proceeded to the railway station.

In the goods yard I found most of my fellow-passengers of the *Seven Seas* and many new faces in addition: all were busy entraining for the north.

The troop train consisted of first class corridor coaches for the officers, second and third-class compartments for N.C.O.'s and men, and cattle-trucks for the horses. In each truck were eight horses, four at each end, packed closely to prevent them falling down. The animals' heads faced a gangway running across the centre of the vehicle. In this space were accommodated the grooms with their arms and accoutrements and forage for their charges. As the weather was very hot, the sliding doors at each end of the gangway were left open.

By 11 a.m. every man and horse was entrained, but as the train showed no immediate intention of starting, several of us left the carriages and went across to a *café* facing the station, where we had an excellent omelette with delicious coffee, hot rolls and butter.

There is a golden rule when campaigning, which is to eat and sleep whenever possible. One can never tell how long the interval may be before the next opportunity presents itself for rest and food.

At 12.10 p.m. the train started. Sharing my compartment were two brother officers of my corps, and as we leant back against the comfortable cushions, a well-filled provision basket at our feet, and gazed through the windows at the lovely scenery we were passing, we remarked with a smile that our present position did not merit the tender sympathy of our people at home, doubtless at that moment imagining we were suffering all the rigours of a campaign.

Little could we guess what was in store, and that in the near future we should be participating in all the horrors attendant upon a retreating army.

At every halt we were met by enthusiastic crowds, chiefly women and young girls, who threw flowers into the carriages and pressed drinks of wine and beer upon the soldiers. Even at stations through which the train passed without stopping, the same crowds were present, bouquets were flung through the windows on to our knees, and our eyes caught a fleeting picture of bright smiling faces, fluttering handkerchiefs, arms full of flowers, and foaming jugs of beer.

The cries of "*Vive l'Angleterre!*" and "*Vivent les Anglais!*" were mingled with demands for souvenirs, to satisfy which the soldiers parted with their cap and collar badges, so that at the end of the day every man had a buttonhole and a sprig of flowers in his cap, but it was impossible to tell to what regiment or corps he belonged.

It was an exceedingly hot day, and we travelled very slowly.

We reached Rouen at 4 p.m., where the train stopped for an hour. Here the French authorities had provided coffee and brandy for the men, and water for the horses.

We reached Amiens at 10 p.m., and had another hour to wait there. During the night we had a tremendous thunderstorm accompanied with heavy rain.

After an uncomfortable night's journey we arrived at a little wayside station called Busigny at 4 a.m. on Friday, 14th August. Here some of the troops were detrained.

We then proceeded to Landrécies at 5 a.m., where more troops detrained, and finally we reached Aulnoye at 7 a.m., which was my destination, and of some half-dozen other officers also of some advance parties.

We were met by the French *commandant*, Major Ferrier, who spoke English fluently, and he arranged for the accommodation of us all in billets in the village. For our meals we joined the French officers in the station buffet, where we were excellently fed for 5 *francs*, which included *déjeûner* and *dîner*.

After a much-needed wash and breakfast Major Browne of the Royal Scots Fusiliers and I proceeded to carry out a reconnaissance of the immediate neighbourhood.

We were the first British to arrive, and our advent caused considerable excitement and interest among the villagers. From these simple-minded, kindly people we received the greatest hospitality; they could not do enough for us, and their kindly interest on our behalf at times almost embarrassed us.

On Saturday and Sunday, 15th and 16th August, we continued the reconnaissance of the country round Aulnoye by motor, and visited Berlaiment, Noyelles, Monceau, Leval, St Remy, and Lamery. At all these places the villagers accorded us a great reception, the girls throwing flowers into the car and presenting us with fruit and bouquets, while the men pressed red and white wine, beer, and even champagne upon us. The drinks we could well have done without, and it was with great difficulty, and only at the risk of giving offence, that we could get away from our hospitable hosts.

At all these villages I made arrangements for the provision of those articles which the soldier and his horse need in billets: fuel, hay, straw, and vegetables. In no single case did any man ask anything above existing prices. Generally negotiations were conducted through the mayor, but in several instances I approached farmers direct, and it reflects the greatest credit on these simple honest folk that they made no attempt to raise the price of those articles which were now demanded in such exceptional quantities.

I wondered whether English or Scottish farmers, in similar circumstances, would have been squeamish about seizing the opportunity proffered by the gods.

A few days later we retired through these same villages, and during those trying days my thoughts often returned to these kindly, inoffensive villagers, and I wondered what must be the fate of the helpless old men and women, and the young, smiling, happy girls, left to the tender mercies of the "frightful" Hun, who would most certainly wreak vengeance upon them for their hospitality to the British Army.

On Monday, 17th August, I motored to Noyelles to meet my brigade, the 9th of the 3rd Division, which had detrained that morning at Landrécies. It arrived at Noyelles during the early afternoon, and was accommodated in *gîtes*—that is, in close temporary billets. Marching with his battalion was an old friend of mine. Lieutenant S—— of the Royal Fusiliers, whom I had known in less stirring times in South Africa. A few days later he met his death most gallantly at Nimy, in the first fight in which our division was engaged.

During the 18th, 19th, and 20th August the concentration of the British Expeditionary Force continued, and on the night of the 20th the orders for the advance next morning were issued.

Our concentration on the night of the 20th had not been com-

17

pleted. Some artillery and engineer units were still missing, and did not join up with the rest of the force until two or three days after the advance had commenced.

Moreover, of the six infantry divisions and one cavalry division which constituted the Expeditionary Force under Lord Haldane's scheme, only four divisions—the 1st, 2nd, 3rd, and 5th—were present with the cavalry division when our forward march began.

The four infantry divisions were organised into two corps. The first was composed of the 1st and 2nd divisions, while the second corps was formed from the 3rd and 5th divisions.

With this attenuated force—in all about 80,000 men—we entered the gigantic arena of battle with nations who numbered their soldiers in millions.

That the *Kaiser* called the British Force a "contemptible little army" there can be no doubt, and the insulting remark loses nothing of its offensiveness by the knowledge that it was true. Contemptible indeed was the British Army; contemptible not on account of its quality—those lionhearted, noble, glorious soldiers who died between Mons and Colummiers, their faces ever to the foe, disproved that fact beyond the shadow of a doubt,—but contemptible because of the paucity of its numbers.

CHAPTER 2

Advance on Mons

On Friday, 21st August, the British Army commenced its march to succour Belgium. We, the 3rd Division, advanced at 6.30 a.m., moving on Longueville, the 5th Division on the right and the First Corps on our left, the cavalry in front.

At 11 a.m. the division reached the neighbourhood of Longueville-Gognies, and went into billets.

The march was a short one, as some of the units had only detrained that morning and joined the division during the day. Headquarters were established in a beautiful old French *château*, situated in the midst of ornamental grounds, not far from Gognies. My own company was camped in an orchard at Longueville, the horses picketed between the trees, the men housed in a big barn, while the officers sheltered under a tarpaulin pulled over two waggons drawn alongside each other.

On Saturday, 22nd August, at 4.15 a.m., the march was continued. We passed through the village of Malplaquet and close under the monument erected by the French people to "The brave of both nations" who fought near by on the 11th September 1709. As I looked round and tried to picture that historic battle, I wondered whether the spirits of the warriors who had slept here for 200 years were watching us as we marched by.

A mile or two farther on we crossed the frontier into Belgium.

At the village of Blarégnies we learned that our advance-guard was in touch with the enemy north of Mons, and that my brigade, the 9th, would probably billet for the night about Cuèsmes.

The delight of the Belgians at seeing our troops was boundless; everywhere we were hailed as deliverers.

It had been a hot dusty march, and, as the men tramped by, the people thrust glasses of beer or water and quantities of fruit into their

Advance on Mons—British troops passing the battlefield and monument of Malplaquet.

hands.

We saw few men of military age, but great numbers of women and children. Business was at a standstill, but the people had not left their homes, and now there seemed no reason why they should do so. Confidence in us was everywhere apparent, and no one had any idea that in a few hours our onward march must develop into a swift retreat.

By 10 p.m. the 9th Brigade, to which I belonged, had reached the line Jemappes-Cuèsmes, and was enjoying rest and food in their billets. One battalion of the Royal Fusiliers was on outpost duty beyond Nimy, to the north of Mons. All day we had heard guns muttering in the distance, and as we lay down and stretched our tired limbs that night we knew that heavy fighting must be expected on the morrow. No dread misgivings, however, assailed us; according to the intelligence reports there were only three German Divisions in front of the British Army.

Sunday, 23rd August, broke—a cold, wet, depressing day. At 3.30 a.m. we rose, stiff and hardly rested from yesterday's labours, and after a hurried breakfast the troops fell in and awaited orders. The Royal Fusiliers were heavily engaged beyond Nimy, and the reports now received proved that our information of yesterday regarding the enemy's strength was far from correct. Instead of three German Divisions, the British Army was faced by five corps—200,000 men—advancing full of confidence after the fall of Liége and Namur. The French on our right and left were retiring, and the British, with flanks *"en l'air,"* were left to meet the whole brunt of the oncoming enemy. The baggage and supply sections of the Train were ordered back at once to Hon, while the battalions of the brigade were directed to take up their allotted positions and put up as stout a resistance as possible.

At this time I received orders to proceed to Mons and see if it were possible to obtain 17,000 rations in the town—to be available should our own supplies fail to reach us. Accordingly I motored into the place, and up through the narrow *pavé* streets to the beautiful town hall standing on one side of a large open square.

Although it was Sunday, and though, too, the sound of the guns and even the rifle fire was distinctly audible, all the shops were open and the streets crowded with people dressed in their best clothes. I admired the town very much, with its clean streets and picturesque buildings, but what astonished me was the holiday appearance of its inhabitants when the enemy was actually knocking at their gates.

Having obtained all the information I required from the mayor and his secretary, I returned to Cuèsmes about 4 p.m., and was surprised to find that the beautiful avenue connecting this suburb with Mons had been transformed during my absence.

Working parties of the Lincolnshire Regiment had cut down many of the splendid trees, and entangled the branches; the *pavé* had been pulled up, and a barricade made across the road, while all approaches were blocked by barbed wire, drain-pipes, or any other handy obstacle.

In Cuèsmes itself other parties were hard at work, assisted by the townspeople. Narrow streets pointing in the direction from which the enemy was expected were wired across, breastworks of *pavé* and carts filled with stone were built across the exits, while on the outskirts the houses were loopholed, and trenches were dug in suitable places in the adjoining fields.

At Jemappes the Royal Scots Fusiliers were similarly occupied, while the space between this place and Cuèsmes was defended by the Northumberland Fusiliers.

About 6 p.m. the Royal Fusiliers were forced to retire from Nimy after a magnificent defence, during which they had had to face six times their numbers.

These preparations for defence made by our troops created consternation among the inhabitants, who had apparently all this time been under the impression that we were going to drive the Germans before us.

To now adopt defensive instead of offensive measures was the first shock, but a still greater surprise was yet in store for these unfortunate people.

The German attack on Jemappes and Cuèsmes was supported by a tremendous artillery fire, the shrapnel raining on the church of the former place like hail. Only after a vigorous resistance, when the enemy was threatening our flanks, did our gallant brigade evacuate these towns, leaving their wounded in the hands of the enemy, and inflicting upon him enormous losses. The German attacks were all made in dense formation, an exceedingly expensive method when employed against highly-trained, well-disciplined, quick and accurate shooting troops such as ours.

About 7 p.m. I received an order to proceed at once to the train and bring up the Supply Section to the troops. After a great deal of searching, and just before dark, I found the train parked in a field beside the road near Hon.

BARRICADING THE STREETS OF CUÈSMES

It was nearly midnight before it was loaded and ready. However, just as we were about to start, we received fresh instructions that the train was to remain at Hon. I then lay down to get a few hours' rest, and at 2 a.m. we were again ordered to proceed to the troops, and as the train commenced its march, I was told to push on and report to Second Corps Headquarters.

I arrived at General Smith-Dorrien s headquarters at Sars-la-Bruyère about 3 a.m. on Monday, 24th August, and was told to immediately return to the train and direct the officer commanding to retire with the utmost despatch towards Beaudignies.

After delivering my message I started to motor back to join my brigade. By this time it was a beautiful bright summer morning, and from a cloudless blue sky the sun shone down on the golden sheaves of corn in the fields, and it was difficult to realise that a bloody battle was raging close by. As I motored on I saw an aeroplane high up, a mere speck in the heavens, and as I gazed at it, tiny clouds of smoke, like fluffs of cotton-wool, appeared all round it where shrapnel shells were bursting. The airman—whether English or German I could not tell at that distance—was flying fast, however, and was soon out of range.

Presently I passed streams of refugees, poor unhappy creatures, walking as fast as possible, dragging tired, frightened children along with them. Some were carrying bundles of clothing and food, others were pushing perambulators in which were babies mixed up with an assortment of domestic articles hurriedly snatched from their homes.

In the British Army they had now ceased to take any interest. They never even glanced at the khaki-clad soldiers. That army in which they had felt such confidence was now fighting for its own existence, and was quite powerless to stop—much less repel—the dread scourge spreading broadcast over Belgium. Added to my feelings of deep pity for the poor women and helpless little ones was an acute sense of humiliation. These women had looked to us to defend them, they had greeted us as deliverers, and in my own case at least I had assured the anxious ones only yesterday that the British Army would never desert them. How could I now look these people in the face? It would have been better for our prestige if we had never entered Belgium at all, rather than to have been kicked out of it, neck and crop, as soon as we met the German forces.

At Frammeries, a small mining town about five miles south of Mons, I found my brigade very hotly engaged with greatly superior numbers. The staff were sheltering on the lee side of some houses in a street running parallel to the German front. Up the streets pointing towards the German position the bullets were flying continuously, knocking up splashes of dust in the road or chipping brick and mortar off the sides of the houses. Overhead was the incessant crack of the shrapnel, and as fast as one group of the little white clouds, caused by the burst of the shells, dissolved into the still morning air, another group appeared. Fortunately the shells were bursting high, and so were not as dangerous as they might have been, but they brought down pieces of chimney-pot, slates, tiles, bricks, and lengths of telegraph wire, which were showered into the streets and about our ears. The continuous rattle of rifle fire, the cracks of the bursting shells, and the discharges of our own artillery, made a babel of noise which I found very distracting. It was wonderful how amidst that pandemonium the brigadier could collect his thoughts, coolly and quickly come to a decision, and quietly issue his orders.

Presently I met an officer of the "Q" branch of the Divisional Headquarters, who informed me that he had just bought all the bread baked during the night in a local bakery, and directed me to secure as much of it as possible and distribute it to the men. Taking my car to a side street, I discovered the bakery just shutting up shop, while a terrified crowd of Belgians were issuing from the premises, each grabbing as many loaves as he could conveniently carry.

With the aid of some half-dozen soldiers I quickly filled the car with the large round flat loaves; then, standing on the running-board, I instructed the chauffeur to keep on that side of the road where the houses afforded some protection.

We proceeded as rapidly as the state of the road would permit, littered as it was with glass, chimney-pots, bricks, and tiles, and I was astonished at the coolness and skill displayed by the driver, a man named Morgan, who had been a chauffeur in London only a few weeks before.

The first groups of soldiers we met were waiting in support under cover of houses and walls; later we turned down towards the barricades or hastily constructed breastworks made from the pave torn up out of the road, and met some companies on their way to reinforce the fighting line, while others were working at a fresh line of barricades to be occupied when the advanced ones could no longer be held. To each I distributed such bread as they wanted: some were glad indeed to get the hot fresh loaves, others were too occupied or too

STAFF OF THE 9TH BRIGADE SHELTERING UNDER A WALL DURING THE ACTION AT FRAMMERIES.

anxious to eat, while most were still in possession of the iron ration carried by every soldier in his haversack to meet such an emergency as the present, when it is impossible or very inadvisable to bring forward the Supply Train.

Presently we were stopped by an officer of the Royal Scots Fusiliers, who said it would be impossible to go farther, as the car would show up above the breastwork, and would immediately draw the enemy's fire. I therefore left it close under cover of a church wall, and ran down to where I perceived a section of artillery in action. I heard the officer in charge giving the range as 600 yards.

The volume of the enemy's artillery and rifle fire here seemed to me terrific; bullets sang over one's head or hissed past one's ears in a continuous stream, while the sound of the battle filled the air like the noise of an army of riveters at work.

I now met small groups of wounded men helping each other along. Presently a doctor, hearing I had a car close by, ran up and inquired whether I would take a badly wounded officer to the hospital. What a splendid fellow that doctor was! With clothes and hands covered in blood, he looked more like a butcher than a surgeon. He seemed wearied to death; he had been where the danger was greatest—wherever a casualty had occurred,—but his one anxiety was to get his patients where they could receive proper attention. The officer whom he wished me to take to hospital was, I think, a subaltern in the 5th Fusiliers, and his shattered arm was a horrid sight. He, however, was too hurt to be moved from the stretcher upon which he lay, so was carried on it up to the hospital.

I then picked up four less seriously wounded men, and took them to the hospital which had been established in the village school. Here in a temporary ward I left them. As I was passing out of the door I paused and looked round. The long room contained a dozen or so beds—some double, some single—dragged in apparently from the nearest houses: there were some mattresses, too, spread on the floor. Immediately on my left was a large double bed in which lay, I supposed, only a slightly wounded man, for he had raised himself on one elbow and was taking a deep interest in the wounded subaltern whom I had been asked to bring up in the car, and who now lay white and still on the stretcher which had been placed on the floor in the centre of the room.

Kneeling beside him was a doctor and two Sisters of Mercy, who, with pity written all over their gentle faces, were assisting the surgeon to remove the clothing and temporary dressings, so that the wound could be properly examined. Across the room on a mattress lay another wounded man, whose eyes were closed, and he lay so still he might have been dead.

Other wounded too were in the building, but as I turned and walked out into the sunshine and noise, I saw only the white face of the wounded officer and the sweet expression on the faces of those Sisters of Mercy, who, quite unmindful of their own danger, seemed only concerned with the suffering that lay all around them.

On returning to the staff, I found they had moved to a new position about 300 yards farther back. They were seated in chairs obtained from a neighbouring house, and placed on the pavement close under the shelter of a high wall. Reports were continually arriving, and the news did not appear too encouraging. In addition to the shrapnel, the Germans were now giving us a taste of their high-explosive shells. The burst of these shells makes a noise that I can only describe as terrifying, and the damage they did to the buildings was far worse than shrapnel was capable of. Except for the noise and the soldiers there was no sign of life in the little town; every door was locked, and every window shuttered. Now and again across the street I noticed a door would open a few inches and a scared face peep out, to disappear again at a warning sign from young H——, the general's staff captain. To analyse one's feelings under heavy fire is, I think, a most interesting study. Personally, my great desire at this time was to appear unconcerned. I would have given much to be anywhere except where I was. The general and his brigade major, I could see, were worried and anxious, and well they might be, considering the difficult and perilous position of the brigade, faced by considerably larger numbers and with no reserve of any kind to fall back upon.

The others all seemed thoughtful, while one of the party started, every time a high explosive shell burst, like a child when one explodes a paper bag behind him.

Some little time before I had sent the car half a mile farther back to get some degree of shelter, and now as the morning wore on we could see it was only a matter of a short time before we should be compelled to fall back. Presently I saw coming up the street towards us some hundreds of our men: the retirement had begun! Gradually those holding the most advanced positions were withdrawn, but not until a fresh line of defence about 400 yards south of the town had been prepared. This line was a length of trench on both sides of the road, and when this was ready and occupied the town was evacuated.

We left our dead and wounded in the hands of the Germans.

The Battle of Mons, which began on the evening of the 22nd and continued till the 24th, though a defeat for the British, can reflect nothing but glory on our arms. The British Army, though sadly lacking correct information of the enemy's movements and strength, greatly outnumbered, weak in artillery, and inadequately supported, put up so magnificent a fight that though driven from all its positions, it yet inflicted on a numerically superior enemy enormous losses, and very severe punishment.

CHAPTER 3

The Retreat

The withdrawal from Frammeries was carried out quietly and in good order. One battalion of the Royal Scots Fusiliers set to work at once, digging trenches just south of the town to cover the retirement and check pursuit, while the remainder of the troops retired to a new position a mile or two farther back.

The men did not appear unduly depressed or fatigued, and there was certainly no sign of demoralisation.

My own duty now was to get into touch as soon as possible with the motor-lorries of the Supply Column and with the horse-drawn vehicles of the Supply Section of the train. I therefore pushed on, taking in the car with me Captain T—— of the Royal Scots Fusiliers, who had been wounded behind the knee and was unable to walk except with great difficulty. After passing through Sars-la-Bruyère I met a staff officer of the division, who instructed me to meet the Supply Section of the train, conduct it to La Boiscrette, and there dump all the supplies on the side of the road, where they would be available for the troops during the retirement, as they would pass that way.

I met the train on its way to La Boiscrette, and on reaching that village found a suitable stretch of grass on the roadside where the supplies were deposited.

My companion T—— was now unable to stand the jolting of the car any farther, and begged to be left at a house in the village, to be picked up by one of the ambulances on the way through. Accordingly I visited house after house, but no one would take in a wounded British officer, for fear, I suppose, that the wrath of the Germans would fall on them for harbouring an enemy. After great difficulty I managed to enlist the pity of an elderly lady and her daughter, who lived in a large house off the road, approached by a short carriage-drive through big iron gates. Here I helped to undress and put T—— to bed, leaving his uniform beside him. I agreed to return and pick him up later, if I possibly could, should by any mischance our troops not retire that way.

Leaving La Boiscrette I met Major D—— of the staff, and together we went to Englefontaine, passing through the small town of Le Quesnoy. This place, Le Quesnoy, had evidently been a fortress in the old days of short-range artillery, and its enormously thick earth ramparts, deep moat and drawbridges, gave it an appearance of strength which under modern conditions it did not possess. No guns were mounted on the ramparts and no soldiers lined the walls; moreover, the town was completely deserted and the houses all shuttered. It gave one an eerie feeling to traverse streets devoid of all human life,—not even a dog or cat was to be seen, every living creature had fled.

After a short wait at Englefontaine we met the supply column and directed it to Beaudignies, where by this time the whole train had also assembled. The operation of transferring loads from the column to the train was just commencing when another staff officer arrived from Division Headquarters. He at once stopped the work, ordered the train to continue the retirement, while the column was to proceed to Bermeries.

It had been a beautiful, bright warm day, but now as night approached the weather changed, heavy clouds gathered overhead, and by the time the supply column reached its destination it was raining heavily and quite dark.

At Bermeries we found the whole division just arriving. It had been marching and fighting hard all day, and the casualties were heavy, my brigade alone having lost 500.

The men were exceedingly cold, wet, hungry, and desperately tired. The village possessed only a very few houses, and could provide no shelter for so many.

The troops, therefore, lay down in the fields or beside the road; their pressing need was sleep, and every other discomfort was forgotten in their craving for rest. To issue supplies to men in such distressed condition is no easy task, even carrying the food from the road to the adjoining fields required effort from the weary fatigue parties. Moreover, in all military operations troops to a more or less extent become intermingled, and to sort out and find units arriving after dark in a strange locality is a work of great difficulty. Stragglers there must be, too, in hundreds; and the shouts of these men inquiring for their battalions, the neighing of horses, rattling of harness, chopping of wood, and the subdued sound of tired men's voices calling to each other, filled the air with a confused hum which brought home to one the fact that thousands of men and horses were all round, though nothing of them could be seen in the darkness.

By midnight the issue of supplies was completed, and my subaltern and I, with the chauffeur, sought sleep in the car, which we drew alongside a stable wall at Amfoiprêt, a mile west of Bermeries.

At 3 a.m. on Tuesday, 25th August, we crawled out of the car, cold, stiff, and aching with cramp. Dawn was just breaking. With a shake and a rub of the eyes with our knuckles we completed our toilet. The next item was breakfast. A little distance away, lying in the road, was a case of preserved meat, and a little farther on another of biscuits. We burst these open by picking them up and letting them fall on to the road. While engaged in this operation I noticed the door of a cottage opposite open, and a staff officer with tousled hair and heavy sleep-laden eyes looked out. He stared at us dully for a moment or two and then disappeared again, shutting the door behind him.

The troops were now stirring, the rain of the night had cleared off, and the sun appeared; thin columns of smoke were rising from the fields as fires were lit for boiling tea. Presently a company of engineers passed, and we, too, then took the road, making for Englefontaine. Here at a wayside *café* we procured a very welcome cup of coffee, bread and butter, and fried some ration bacon on the stove.

We also examined the car carefully, as we had been too busy the day before to do so. We found that it had been struck in two places either by bullets or shrapnel balls. The damage fortunately was slight, and had not touched the engine. It had probably been done at Frammeries the morning before.

We had been unable the previous night to obtain any orders as to our destination to-day, and we questioned small bodies of troops now passing us making towards Le Cateau. They also were without instructions, but had an idea the retreat was being continued in a south-westerly direction. I did obtain, however, some news which caused me considerable anxiety—namely, that no troops of our division had passed through La Boiscrette the evening before. I thought of my friend T—— whom I had left at that place, and my promise to him that I would return and pick him up if I possibly could do so. To have gone to La Boiscrette the night before was out of the question, as my duty claimed me till midnight; moreover, I had then no grounds for assuming that troops would not pass his way, considering the supplies had been dumped there for their express use the day before. To go now was impossible, as the village was already occupied by the Germans.

With a heavy heart I joined the masses of troops now passing along the road to Le Cateau.

About 11 a.m. we entered this small town. A portion of General Headquarters still remained, and I reported there and obtained some useful information with regard to the general situation.

The little square of the town was filled with cars, staff officers were hurrying to and fro, while troops, both French and English, were pouring through in one continuous stream. Sauntering quietly across the square were Mr Seely and the Duke of Westminster, the former dressed as a colonel on the staff.

Across the square facing the town hall was a little *café* which was still open, though all the shops and private houses were now locking their doors and shuttering the windows. At the entrance to this *café* I noticed a woman who had been standing perfectly still, watching all that was taking place, ever since I had entered the town. She was tall, slight, and well-dressed, with dark hair and eyes, good features, but pale complexion. She attracted attention because she was the only woman to be seen, and, moreover, was the only individual among all the people in the square who seemed in no way disturbed or excited. Apparently, too, she had no intention of leaving the town. She watched with more than interest the passage of the troops, and scanned every officer, French or English. She spoke, however, to no one, and apparently knew nobody.

I wondered who she was, and what she was doing in this little town at such a time; and when every one else had either left the place or was taking hurried steps to do so, why she should be the sole exception.

Was she a spy? Had she come here, where General Headquarters had been established, to obtain all the information possible about the British forces, and was she now only waiting for the Germans to arrive to give them the details?

My conjectures were suddenly disturbed by a rapid burst of fire from an anti-aircraft gun in the square, mounted on a car, and directed by a French officer in brown uniform, upon a German aeroplane of the Albatross type sailing overhead. Several soldiers took up the firing with their rifles, and the horrid din created by the discharges continued for some minutes until the aeroplane soared gracefully out of view, apparently none the worse for the stream of lead directed at it.

Looking towards the *café*, I saw the mysterious woman still there, seemingly quite undisturbed by the noise and excitement. We proceeded out of Le Cateau by the road which rises to the ridge behind the town and then continues in a straight line along the crest of the ridge through Inchy and Beaumont to the little town of Caudry. Along the summit of the ridge hundreds of civilian labourers were hurriedly digging trenches, and the prevailing impression was that the retreat was over, and that the British Army would take up a position along the ridge, and thus advantageously posted fight a big battle.

The day had been hot and dusty, and out beyond Caudry a large force of French cavalry was rapidly moving, raising great clouds of dust.

From the ridge a magnificent view to the north is obtained, and the hot sun shone down on the farms and little villages scattered over the valley and upon the golden sheaves of corn standing in rows like soldiers across the fields.

Along the winding roads appeared masses of troops marching towards the ridge, while beyond them, far out over the crest of the distant hills, rose columns of dust proclaiming the presence of more, and still more, troops on the march.

At 4 p.m. a violent thunderstorm broke, and the rain falling in a deluge speedily soaked every one to the skin.

At nightfall the supply column arrived, and I was ordered to take five of the lorries with supplies to my brigade, which I should find at Troisville. I reached there in the pitchy darkness at 11 p.m., to find not a vestige of life in the place. Not a light was to be seen, every house was deserted, not even a dog barked. Leaving the vehicles near a church I proceeded to reconnoitre on foot; my footsteps were the only sounds that disturbed the stillness. Past the houses I came upon the fields, and leaving the road tramped across the ploughed land towards a light I saw in the distance.

Suddenly a challenge rang out, followed by the crack of a rifle and the shrill crescendo of a bullet screaming into the darkness. "Friend!" I shouted, and looking round, discerned the dark figure of a sentry standing in the shadow of a hedge. Being bidden to pass, I remonstrated with the man in no measured terms. It appeared, however, that he had already challenged once and had received no reply. After this I remained on the road, taking no further chances across country, and came at last to the headquarters of the 13th Brigade. They, however, could give me no news of my own brigade.

There was nothing to be done but return. I reached Troisville again, but there lost myself in a maze of streets. I seemed to find dozens of churches, but not the one where I had left the vehicles. Suddenly, to my delight, I heard the rapid beats of a motor-cycle engine, and a despatch-rider appeared round a corner. Taking me up on his carrier we quickly found the lorries, the drivers of whom were by now considerably anxious over my long absence. Returning to Bertry I reported at Division Headquarters at 1 a.m. on the 26th. Round the sides of a long shed at the back of a church officers and men were lying on straw, worn out by their continuous exertions. In the middle of the room at a table sat the general dictating a despatch in a low voice to a staff officer.

The light of a lamp fell on the general's fine soldierly features; his face was drawn with fatigue and anxiety. The despatch finished, the general uttered a name in the same low voice; immediately one of the staff officers lying round the room rose to his feet, put on his cap, took up the despatch from the table, saluted, and, passing out of the door, disappeared into the night.

Turning to me the general asked my business, and being informed, pointed out on the map the town of Inchy, where my brigade would be found. Again I started out into the night, and this time with success. The troops were in Inchy, the wearied men lying on the pavements or in the road, and too exhausted even to hear the approaching vehicles. Stopping the lorries, the drivers and I had to descend and make a path through the slumbering forms by literally dragging their bodies on to the pavements or sides of the road.

At the junction of three streets by Brigade Headquarters we deposited the supplies in the midst of hundreds of sleeping soldiers, and at 4.30 a.m., as the sun was appearing, we returned to the Train Headquarters at Montigny, after 25½ hours' consecutive duty. I lay down to snatch a short rest.

It seemed to me that I had hardly closed my eyes when K—— and T—— roused me, saying the troops were already on the march, and that the train was ordered to St Quentin.

It was 6 o'clock, a fine morning, but the roads still wet from the previous night's rain.

We were all much depressed to find the retreat was to be continued, and also very tired.

Making a hurried breakfast of milk and bread, which was all we could get, we started off for St Quentin. The roads were thronged with troops, and we passed large numbers of villagers, terrified and in tears, flying with such household goods and chattels as they were able to carry.

We reached St Quentin about two in the afternoon. The shops were open, and most of the inhabitants gathered in the streets. The people, however, were decidedly unfriendly in their attitude to the British—a new experience for us after the invariable courtesy and kindness we had received up to date from the French people.

Such, however, is the way of the world: friends in distress are rarely welcome guests, and often are a source of embarrassment.

From General Headquarters I received an order to meet the supply column coming from Peronne and take it to my division at Estrées. The road via Le Catelet was not to be followed, as parties of Uhlans were reported on it, but I was to turn off to the right about six miles south of Le Catelet. Every precaution was to be taken to meet attack and to beat off such small bodies of enemy cavalry as we might chance to meet on the way.

As soon as the twenty seven lorries of the column arrived about six in the evening, I disposed all the armed men to the best advantage. Sangars of sacks of oats were built round every fourth or fifth vehicle. Within these breastworks were placed as many men as could conveniently handle their rifles, and in each of these travelling forts was an officer, while another officer sat beside the leading driver.

Except for the officers and N.C.O.'s, all the men were specially enlisted—that is, they had been only a very short time before motor-omnibus and lorry drivers in civilian life. Better men one could not desire. On this occasion they were splendid. Though they had been working for the past five days and nights twenty-two hours out of twenty four, snatching sleep and food at odd moments, often employed on most trying and dangerous duties and sometimes under shell and rifle fire, yet never a word of grumbling did I hear, and every order was obeyed with an alacrity and a cheerfulness of spirit that would have done credit to veteran soldiers.

At dusk we started taking the splendid broad tree-lined north road, and made good progress till 8.30 p.m., when through the darkness we suddenly saw the road ahead crowded with a mass of troops. I saw they were all infantrymen, and thereby guessed they must be our own people. Presently we reached them, and our farther progress was stopped. They were in no military order, and without officers or senior N.C.O.'s,—obviously stragglers, with a few wounded limping along in their midst, representatives of a dozen different regiments from two or three Divisions. In number they must have been three or four hundred. Some of them said that the enemy were close at their heels—in fact, were even at that moment in ambush about half a mile farther on in a thick wood bordering the road.

If their story was true I was in an unpleasant predicament. A tree laid across the road or a volley fired into the engine of the leading lorry would finish all chances of a dash through, while from the dark depths of the wood the enemy's marksmen would in comparative safety pick off my people exposed on the road.

However, my orders were to get to my division, so there was nothing to be done but get on.

All the headlights were lit in the hope that their glare would upset the enemy's markmanship, and would also show up any obstruction in the road. In addition, I took up about thirty men from the stragglers who were armed, and distributed them over the convoy.

Then, telling the leading lorry driver to go at his best speed and the others to follow, I clambered into the first sangar and away we thundered into the darkness. The roar of the rapidly moving vehicles, the blackness of the night, the proximity of the enemy, and our grave anxiety concerning the fate of our own division struggling in the obscurity ahead with ten times its number of enemies, all combined to keep us in the highest state of tension.

Approaching the wood, which we could now discern looking like a great dark wall beside the road, we prepared to return the fire which we momentarily expected to issue from it. Not a sight nor sound of an enemy appeared, however, from its depths, and in a few moments we had passed through it, and, breathing a sigh of relief, slowed down to a more moderate speed. In time we reached the turning to our right which we had to follow, and leaving the broad highroad, we now found we were in a country lane. Suddenly round a corner came the head of an advancing column of troops. It was the British —— Division retiring under cover of night. In the narrow road the advancing columns stopped our further progress, and we pulled the heavy lorries as far to one side of the way as we could to let the tired men get past,—infantry staggering along in utter weariness, horsemen lying asleep on their horses' necks, cyclists pushing their machines; with constant checks and breaking of ranks, horse, foot, and artillery went slowly by, an interminable stream of shadows. To add to the difficulty and discomfort it commenced to rain, making the foothold on the road slippery and treacherous.

Presently some staff officers rode up, and in excited language demanded to know why I was blocking the road. They demanded that the lorries should be flung into the ditch so as not to impede further the retirement of the troops. My expostulations were fortunately heard by a general officer, who in quiet cool tones informed me that I must give up all idea of getting through to Estrées, as the roads leading up to that place were blocked with troops, but that I should turn the lorries at the next cross-roads two hundred yards farther on and take them back to St Quentin. Slowly and with great difficulty this was accomplished, and though our mission to the 3rd Division had to remain unfulfilled, yet some measure of good was done, for supplies were distributed to the men of the division now struggling past, who were greatly in need of them.

We arrived back at St Quentin at 3 a.m. on the 27th, and sought a couple of hours' rest.

At 6 a.m. we were again on the move. In the square I met one of the divisional staff, whom I assisted in directing through the town the masses of troops now pouring into it from the north.

Regiment after regiment, battery after battery filed past. Gone was all the smartness and proud bearing of troops on parade: these dirty, unkempt, weary, footsore soldiers tramped along in silence, their eyes on the ground, their uniforms torn and mud-stained, just a stream of desperately tired, sorely suffering humanity.

What dangers and privations had they not passed through during the last five days!

Singled out for destruction by a numerically far superior enemy, they had been attacked incessantly night and day without respite for rest or food; rained upon .with shot and shell, and forced to retire from one position to another in wet and cold, heat and dust, yet in spite of all the spirit of these splendid soldiers was still unbroken. Time and again had they turned on their gigantic pursuer. At Le Cateau the day before they had rent his leading ranks and left his dead in thousands strewing the fields, and though battered and worn they had yet caused him to pause dismayed, until he could bring fresh legions forward to renew the attack.

As I watched these men I reflected that had Britain placed a million such as they, instead of a mere handful, into Belgium at the opening of the campaign, on her would have been shed the undying glory of having saved that unfortunate little country from the ruthless savagery of the German hosts. Those atrocities which have made the world shudder would then have never added another crimson page to history.

CHAPTER 4

The Retreat Continued

The retreat was continued through Roupy to Ham, where the troops commenced to arrive about 1 p.m. on the 27th. Never have I seen men so tired. From St Quentin to Ham the road was lined with hundreds who had dropped out of the ranks too exhausted to continue the march. Some of these must have fallen into the hands of the enemy, but many managed to struggle on after a short rest. The little town of Ham lies at the foot of a valley, and is completely commanded by the high ground to the north, through which runs the road from St Quentin.

As the guns and regimental transport slowly descended the hill and entered Ham, we expected every moment that the enemy's artillery would shell the little town and add to the great difficulty of getting the tired men and animals through the narrow streets. Our rearguard, however, held the enemy back, and the main body of our troops crossed the Somme and bivouacked in the fields south of Ham for a few hours. The staff remained in the town, from which most of the inhabitants had fled in the morning. I was billeted with three other officers in a fine mansion, where the housekeeper and butler, who had been left to take care of the house, did all they could to make us comfortable. A splendid bedroom was assigned to each of us, and the snowy linen sheets and frilled pillow-cases looked very inviting in our dusty weary condition.

How I longed to get in between those soft sheets and put in a good eight hours' sleep! I had almost forgotten what a bed felt like, as I had not even taken my coat off for seven days and nights. At seven o'clock, just as I was sitting down to an excellent dinner prepared by the housekeeper, I was sent for by Corps Headquarters, and a staff officer gave me an order to proceed to St Quentin and see if the supply column was there. No one knew what had become of it since it left that town in the early morning, and it was thought possible that after filling up with supplies at Peronne it might have returned to St Quentin.

It seemed to me rather an absurd order, as it was common knowledge that the Germans had entered St Quentin about 5 p.m. However, there was nothing for me to do but obey.

With an appetite quite spoilt I returned to my dinner, determined at any rate to try and have a square meal before starting on what might be my last journey. I felt sorry for the chauffeur, but had to take him, as I could not drive the car myself, an art which I now greatly regretted I had not learned. After a good dinner and a bottle of wine we started up the engine, and, taking my seat beside the driver, we slipped away into the rain and darkness.

Just out of the town we met a car followed by a number of lorries, and to my inexpressible relief discovered that this was the missing supply column turned up at last from Peronne.

I returned with the news to the staff officer who had despatched me on my mission, who on seeing me greeted me with the words, "Hallo! you've come back. I didn't expect to see you or the car again."

What a charming fellow, I thought, to despatch me on an errand from which he never expected me to return!

Orders were now received stating that the retirement was to be continued at midnight. No chance now of that soft bed! I returned to the billet and packed up my few belongings. The housekeeper and the butler were dreadfully upset on seeing our preparations for departure, and the former wept noisily. I recommended them to lock up the house and seek a healthier locality, and left them collecting such few things as they could take with them.

Poor creatures, how sorry we felt for them! We had enjoyed their hospitality, but were powerless to protect them.

At about 3 a.m. on the 28th we reached Noyon. Here we were fortunate enough to get beds in a nunnery. All the nuns had long since left, but the Mother Superior and two or three other sweet-faced gentle women had remained behind in the huge empty building. In some of the clean but scantily furnished cells were iron cots, now occupied by war-worn dusty officers instead of the quiet nuns. In the next cell to mine were two staff officers. How thankful we were to rest our weary limbs, and the coarse sheets, hard beds, and bare whitewashed walls appeared luxury indeed.

At 6 a.m. we awoke much refreshed, and after coffee and bread and butter took the car to Mouille, where the main body of the division had bivouacked for the night. The news from the Staff was not too cheerful—the Germans still pressing hard on our heels. However, by 9 a.m. the whole situation changed, the German pressure being relaxed, and it was assumed that the long-looked-for assistance of the French had at last arrived. The destruction of the bridge over the river at Ham by our engineers the previous evening also no doubt checked the enemy's pursuit.

At any rate our troops were not molested during the march, and the short rest they had had at Mouille had done them good. I walked with the battalions for some miles, and it was difficult to recognise in these men, marching easily and cheerily along under the shade of the trees on each side of the road, the same soldiers whom I had seen in such miserable plight only the day before.

The morale of the British Army has always been exceptionally high, and this combined with an excellent discipline now proved its great value. A few hours' complete rest and an opportunity for obtaining food had put the troops once again into high fettle, their confidence in themselves had returned, and once more they were capable of giving an excellent account of themselves.

To my great delight I heard that T——, who had been wounded at Frammeries and whom I had taken in my car and left at La Boiscrette on the 24th, had rejoined his battalion. He had been picked up by an ambulance waggon of the 5th Division which had passed that way the same afternoon.

The main approach to Noyon was much congested by troops and transport, the 3rd, 4th, and 5th Divisions all using the same road. The main body of the 3rd Division bivouacked just north of the town, the 9th Brigade being at Croiselles, the other brigades at Genvry and Pontoise.

That night I slept in a little cottage standing beside the road. It was about two in the morning of the 29th before my work permitted me to seek some rest, but even at this hour the good woman of the cottage prepared some hot coffee and eggs for my subaltern and myself. The kitchen was evidently both the living and sleeping room, for there was a bed in the corner on which I spread my valise, while my subaltern slept on the kitchen table. At 7 a.m., before leaving, we again partook of the cottager's hospitality, and though her husband was probably only a labourer in the fields in normal times and now a private soldier, yet she absolutely refused to accept any payment for the food and lodging she had provided. Such kindness and hospitality given by the poorest peasants of France to the soldiers of England was common enough at this time.

This day, 29th August, was an easy day for the troops. The enemy beyond the Somme was busy bridging the river, and the respite thus given to our troops was most welcome.

I motored through the beautiful forest road to Compiègne, where the supply column was being loaded. Compiègne at this time was the Headquarters of the British Army, and a very picturesque town it is, with its wide *pavé* streets, large open squares, and fine buildings.

On returning to my division I found that Divisional Headquarters had been established in a beautiful country house, the Château Cuts, standing in a huge park about four miles south-east of Noyon. I thought it a thousand pities that this lovely place, with its pointed gables, terraced walks, and prettily laid out flower-gardens should be left to the mercies of the Hun. Late that night I went up to the Chateau for orders, and the lights from the windows reflected into the waters of the moat surrounding the house made it look like a fairy palace.

Entering the mansion, I found several officers snatching a few hours' sleep in long cane chairs in the hall. Off this hall was a large room, round the sides of which a dozen or more beds without bedding were ranged. Stretched upon the mattresses on these beds were officers and orderlies, booted and spurred, deep in the slumber they so much needed. In the dining-room the table was spread with food and drink for those who had time to snatch it. In another room the general and a few of his staff were poring over maps and writing orders.

I found that we were to march at 2 a.m. next morning, the 30th. After taking a snack of supper at the *château* I turned into the car for a couple of hours' sleep, and at 2 a.m. we were again on the move through Marbay and Nampsel by the road running over the hills. My own brigade marched by the valley road through Morsain, where I met it about 9 a.m. while it was halted for a short rest. Leaving my subaltern at Morsain to requisition supplies for the brigade, I proceeded with a staff officer of the division to Berny Rivière to make arrangements for the arrival of the troops there that evening.

I had much to do, and it was not until long after dark, when all the troops were in, that I discovered my subaltern S—— was missing. No one appeared to have seen him since Morsain, but that he would have been so foolish as to remain there after the troops had left I could not believe, as the country in our rear was swarming with Uhlans only too ready to pounce upon any straggler.

As the night wore on and there was still no word of him, my anxiety on his behalf increased.

At 5 a.m. next morning I received a message from Divisional Headquarters saying that he had telephoned in from Morsain asking to be fetched at once, as bodies of Uhlans were in the neighbourhood. This little village nestled at the foot of the hills six miles outside our outposts, and we pushed the car to its best speed along the winding valley road. Every moment I expected to round a bend and find a patrol of Uhlans blocking the way.

At Morsain, standing in the middle of the deserted main street, was S——, anxiety written all over his countenance, which changed to relief when he recognised me.

We wasted no time in turning the car, and returned as fast as we had come to Berny Rivière, while S—— narrated his adventures of the night before.

It appeared that on the previous day, while he was paying for the supplies he had requisitioned, the troops had gone on, so too had his horse; moreover, when his payments were completed the troops were out of sight, and he had no idea which way they had taken.

Just before dark a troop of the hussars from the British Cavalry Corps entered Morsain. He joined them, and they spent the night in a large house just off the main road, which they barricaded across. During the night the barricade and *château* were reconnoitred by several parties of Uhlans, shots were exchanged, and at least one Prussian was believed to have been killed. At dawn the hussars had left Morsain, and having no spare horses were forced to leave S—— to his fate. A telephone was, however, in the village, deserted now by all its inhabitants, and on placing the receiver to his ear he was overjoyed to receive a reply, and managed after some difficulty to get into communication with the Divisional Headquarters.

At 7.30 a.m. on the 31st, after an excellent night's rest, the march was resumed from Brény to Crépy-en-Valois, a dirty town, and on the following day, Tuesday, the 1st September, Penchard, about three miles north of Meaux, was reached. Meaux is rather a fine town, but was on this day deserted, the houses shuttered, the shops closed, and, except for a few *gendarmes* at the gates, showed no sign of life. My subaltern and I managed to obtain here a considerable quantity of tobacco for the use of the troops, but as it was too late then to take it out to the brigade, we spent the night in the town. We were billeted in the house of the *directeur* of the college, a fine mansion beautifully furnished, and for the first time since 21st August I took off my clothes and slept in pyjamas between sheets in a delightfully comfortable bed. After a bath next morning and a breakfast from such scraps as we could find in the deserted house we rejoined the division, which rested for the day in and about the villages of Penchard, Monthyon, and Neufmontiers.

About 7 in the evening, after I had finished issuing supplies to my brigade, I was ordered with other supply officers to report to the train at Lèches. This village was not clearly marked on our maps, and after searching till 11 p.m. we failed to find either Lèches or the train, so decided to spend the night on the roadside. The car was pulled on to the grass, where S—— also laid his valise, and after some supper we turned in for a few hours' rest. The cold and the dust raised in clouds by passing lorries and motorcycle despatch-riders made it an uncomfortable night, and at 4 a.m. on 3rd September, stiff with cold and feeling very dirty, I crawled out of the car. The sun rose soon after, and its beams shining through the trees fell on the hoar-frost in the fields, making the grass appear as if strewn with myriad diamonds.

Taking the road once more we crossed the Marne near Esbly and proceeded towards Jôssigny, where we knew the supply column would rendezvous. Between Serris and Jôssigny we passed the flying ground and headquarters of the Royal Flying Corps, and stopped a moment to watch this splendid corps commencing its day's work. One or two machines had already been up observing the pilot and observer in helmet and goggles in their seats, mechanics holding the tips of the planes while another was turning the huge propeller so as to start the engine. In a moment or two, with a roar as the engine fired, the machine raced swiftly over the earth, and then, increasing its speed, rose gracefully into the still morning air like some huge bird, showing as it circled over our heads the Union Jack of Old England and the Tricolour of France painted on the under-surface of its wings.

The value of the information gained by our intrepid airmen throughout the retreat was incalculable, and the courage, endurance, readiness of resource and daring which they have displayed on all occasions, proves that our air service is second to none in the world.

On arriving at Jôssigny we met the supply column, and with other supply officers had breakfast in the grounds of a *château* nearby. Afterwards we again proceeded in search of the train, and succeeded in daylight where we had failed at night—running it to earth between

A.S.C. OFFICERS BREAKFASTING IN THE GROUNDS OF A *CHÂTEAU* AT JOSSIGNY.

Lèches and Coupvray. It was drawn up in a field beside the road, the horses hooked in, the drivers in their seats all ready for moving off when the orders arrived. These were now received, and the train was directed to march on Crécy *via* Coutevroult.

The retreat, which had up to date been in rather a south-westerly direction towards Paris, now changed direction to the southeast, and as we mounted the high ground above Crécy we could see the valley of the Marne behind and below us, with the river winding like a blue ribbon between its wooded banks.

Rumours and conjectures were rife this day. At one moment we heard that we were going to take up a strong position overlooking the Marne and fight a battle to dispute the passage of that river by the German forces; the next moment it was certain that the retreat would be continued, and that the British Army would recoup and refit within the defences of Paris. Yet another story was that Paris was to be left to its fate, that both French and British field armies would retire into the heart of France and there await an opportunity to shatter the forces of Germany.

Whatever may have been the cause of the rumours, there is no doubt that the fate of Paris hung in the balance on this day, and that there were at this time many people in France who considered it hopeless to prolong the struggle, that Paris must fall, and that the events of 1870-71 would be repeated with even more tragic result.

The enemy's airmen were particularly busy on this afternoon, several of their machines being visible in the air at the same time. One Taube flew low along our lines, drawing a tremendous rifle fire, which, however, seemed to take no effect, for he continued serenely on his way, finally disappearing over the treetops towards the Marne.

The next morning, 4th September, we were up as usual with the dawn, and at 7.30 a.m. were again on the march through Crécy and Tigeaux.

The Germans, however, were not permitted to cross the Marne with impunity; very heavy fighting took place, and our artillery, with that of the French, poured a tremendous fire on the enemy as he crossed the river. The discharge of the guns was so rapid and sustained that they resembled in sound a continuous roll of thunder.

The retreat was continued through the Forest of Crécy, and at midnight the supply column and train waggons met at the Obélisque, in the heart of the forest, and transferred their loads.

This obelisk, a tall slender pillar of stone, stands at the junction of

THIRD DIVISION TRAIN AT LÈCHES.

six straight roads, and forms, as it were, the hub of a giant wheel, the roads spreading like spokes through the dark forest.

Lighting a fire on the grass at the edge of the trees we lay down beside it and cooked ourselves some supper. Around us was the black curtain of the trees, overhead a brilliant star-spangled sky, while along the pale dusty road marched the troops, an endless procession of ghostly figures, the continuous tramp of thousands of feet being broken now and again by the jingle of harness, the champing of a bit, and the rattle of wheels.

When all except the rearguard had marched by we completed the transference of loads, the supply lorries then disappeared down one long avenue between the trees, while we followed the way taken by the troops.

At 3.30 a.m. on the 5th we reached the little village of Chartres, and I lay down under a waggon for a few hours' sleep. Later in the day I went on to Liverdy, where my brigade was billeted, and after issuing supplies from the waggons continued on to Villepayen, where the whole train was now assembled. In the evening I went to Chaumes, and then on to Lieusaint to meet the supply column and guide it to Villepayen, finding great difficulty in locating that village in the dark.

Much of our work had of late been performed at night, and even with the best maps it is a most difficult matter to find one's way in a strange country after dark. In daylight there are many landmarks that can be seen and compared with the map, and one can thereby assure one's position with a considerable degree of accuracy. At night, however, one is surrounded by a pall of darkness, vision is restricted to a radius of a few yards, and one's position must always be a matter of guesswork until some prominent object easily recognisable both on the ground and on the map is reached.

On arrival at Villepayen I found every one in great spirits. The retreat was actually over, and the advance was to commence on the following day.

No wonder we were elated. The retirement from Belgium was a nightmare which we should not easily forget. But it was over now; we could turn over that black page and start a clean sheet.

The retreat of the British Army from Mons, followed by its immediate and brilliant participation in the operations on the Marne and the Aisne, will go down to history as one of the greatest of its military achievements, comparable with the retreat to and victory of Corunna.

CHAPTER 5

The Marne

The advance commenced early on the morning of Saturday, the 6th September, the troops marching hard towards the north-east. My duty sent me in the opposite direction towards Lieusaint, where in the evening I met the motor-lorries of the supply column and accompanied them to a prearranged rendezvous, where we arrived about 10 p.m. It had been arranged that a staff officer from the division should meet us at this rendezvous and guide us in the direction taken by the troops. On our arrival, however, no staff officer was to be seen, and as the time passed and he still failed to appear, the officer commanding the Column and I grew more and more perplexed as to what course of action to pursue.

We had not been told the troops' objective, and we knew that the distance they advanced and the direction they took must depend largely on the enemy.

In front of us, and spreading to right and left as far as the eye could reach, was the Forest of Crécy. If the supply column left the rendezvous and entered the forest it would make it very difficult for the staff officer to find us.

At 11.30 p.m., as no representative from the division had put in an appearance, we left the motor vehicles at the rendezvous and proceeded ourselves in search of the troops. C——, the officer in command of the column, took one road in his car, I took another, while a motor cyclist was sent in a third direction. Through the dark forest road I went to the obelisk, from there to the edge of the Bois d'Hautefeuille, skirting Lord Rothschild's magnificent estate, then back through Fontenay to the column, where I arrived at 2 a.m. on the 7th without encountering any sign of the troops, and found the others had also returned equally unsuccessful.

At 4 a.m. I started off again in the car in search of the division, and at 7 a.m., while flying down one of the roads cut through the Bois d'Hautefeuille, very narrowly escaped collision with another car which was dashing along another forest avenue at right angles to the road I was taking. As we both jammed on the brakes I recognised in one of the occupants of the other car the missing staff officer.

Our delight at seeing each other was mutual. He had been searching for the supply column all night. He had lost the note-book in which he had made an entry of the spot fixed for the rendezvous, nor could he recollect the place, having many other matters to think of.

The headquarters of the division were established in the deserted Château Hautefeuille, the troops resting in the fields around.

To bring up the Supply Column and issue the supplies to the brigades did not take long.

The *château* of Hautefeuille, the shooting-box of a French cavalry officer married to an American millionairess, stands in the midst of lovely country. The house was most luxuriously fitted: every bedroom had its own bathroom, and on each large marble toilet-table was a perfect regiment of cut-glass gold-stoppered bottles containing perfumes, washes, bay rum, and *eau de Cologne.*

In the afternoon, after revelling in the luxury of a bath, I retired for a couple of hours' sleep, and in the depths of a satin eider-down, under a canopy of silk, was soon deep in the slumber I had forgone for thirty hours.

Later on I strolled through the corridors and into the deserted apartments of this palatial shooting box, examining with interest the beautiful panelling and tapestries on the walls, the soft thick carpets under foot, and the exquisite furniture and appointments of the rooms.

Everything in this house was in perfect order, exactly as the owners had left it—the clothes folded up and laid neatly in the presses, toilet bottles and brushes in their appointed places, and even the beds, with their spotless linen sheets, embroidered pillow-cases, and silk and satin coverings awaiting their occupants. The German advance-guard had occupied the mansion for a night, and I was astonished beyond measure to see that the mannerless Hun had left here none of the marks of his beastly "*Kultur.*"

American dollars had built and furnished this diminutive palace, and perhaps the knowledge of this fact had restrained the barbarians from wantonly destroying any of the furniture or effects which the house contained.

Leaving with regret the soft comforts of peace, I joined the troops now preparing to resume the advance.

Motorcars of staff officers were hurriedly leaving one after the other, horses picketed on the smooth lawns under the trees were being hastily saddled, and soldiers who had been resting their tired limbs in the shade were now rising, adjusting their packs and looking to their rifles.

Turning our backs on the *château* we set our faces towards Coulommiers. Through the Bois d'Hautefeuille the columns wound, frightening the pheasants from the coverts beside the road.

At the corner of a wood we passed the bodies of three French soldiers, who had been killed during the German advance, and were still lying unburied in their native woods.

About 8 in the evening the train reached Mortceuf, and the villagers turned out with their horses to help our waggons through the deep ravine in which the hamlet lies, and up the steep acclivity beyond. Later, the mayor pressed me to partake of a hurried supper, and sitting in the chair which had been occupied the previous night by the Prussian general Von Pasnitz, I enjoyed some chicken and a bottle of wine, while my host described how the crown prince's famous Death's Head Hussars had occupied the village the evening before. Today they had been driven out by our cavalry, and had left behind them their dead, who now lay still enough in the orchards and flower-gardens of Mortceuf and in the woods on the heights above.

About midnight I arrived at Coulommiers, and after seeing that the troops had received their supplies, entered a large house in the square with other supply officers to spend the rest of the night.

The doors stood wide open, straw in large quantities covered the floor of the hall, the front room, the stairs, and the landing above, while at every step my feet tripped over or kicked an empty bottle. In the dining-room on the table lay the remains of a meal, scraps of bread and meat, dirty plates and knives, and innumerable empty bottles, chiefly champagne.

As we stood and surveyed, by the light of a guttering candle, the mess around us, a frightened-looking woman entered the house and informed us that this was her master's house, a doctor of the town, and that it had been occupied for the last two or three days by the enemy. The Prussian general had made it his headquarters, and he and his staff had barely completed their meal that evening when the British burst into the town, driving him and his troops before them.

During the occupation of Coulommiers the Germans had drunk every bottle of champagne in the place, and judging by the number empty then strewing the floor, they must have poured the golden wine in copious quantities down their throats.

In the drawing-room the bookcase and writing-desk had been broken open and their contents strewn over the floor. Upstairs the bedclothes lay in untidy heaps on the beds, while chests of drawers and wardrobes had been ransacked and clothing lay littered in every direction.

We opened the windows to let out some of the odour of unwashed humanity that oozed from the straw, and lay down on the beds, only too glad in our wearied state to get a soft spot to lie on.

At 5 o'clock on the morning of the 8th September we were ready once more, and the advance was continued, heavy fighting taking place as our troops followed hard in the wake of the retiring Germans.

The first prisoner made by the division, a Prussian infantry soldier, was, I believe, taken by the Army Service Corps. He was detected skulking in a wood alongside the road, and rounded up after a short chase. He seemed about twenty-four years of age, fair and healthy looking, his body well clothed and nourished. Seated on a waggon beside the driver he now tried to appear perfectly at ease, although surrounded by a circle of faces gazing with curiosity at the first German in uniform they had seen. At every village which we passed through the inhabitants yelled with rage when they saw him, shaking their fists and making significant gestures with their fingers across their throats.

I quite understood their feelings somewhat later, when I had positive proof of the villainies committed by the Prussians.

Through Orly the advance continued, the rattle of rifle fire and the sharp crack of the shrapnel getting louder and more incessant as our troops harried the Prussian rearguard. Presently Bussières was reached as the evening fell, and on the road and in the fields and woods around lay the evidences of the German rout—broken waggons, motor lorries and dead horses strewed the way, while in the fields and in the dark woods lay the dead and the wounded. Many of the latter were brought in by us, some desperately hurt, one an officer with a badly shattered leg, his clothes drenched with blood and the death agony written on his white drawn face.

On through the dark horrid night we pressed to Les Feuchères, passing through more German dead and wounded, their white faces and ghastly forms dimly discernible through the blackness in the fields beside the road. Just before reaching the village our attention was attracted by groans from a wood near by. With an electric torch S——— searched the ground, and seven more of our enemies did we bring in to the shelter and care of our ambulances. Two were officers, one slightly wounded, while the other had a shrapnel ball in his chest.

About Les Feuchères the main body of the division halted, but my brigade had been the advance-guard and was a mile or two ahead, and there in the early hours of the 9th September my company arrived. We found the troops, exhausted by their efforts, lying in the road and adjoining meadows; fires had been lit but had now burned low, leaving only the glowing red embers.

At dawn we were up once more; the troops fell in, the artillery rattled past, and as the light grew we saw we were on the heights overlooking the Marne, and there, down by the blue river and through the wooded hills beyond, streamed huge dark columns of the enemy. Presently the air echoed with the discharges of our field artillery and the quick *rat-tat-tat* of the machine-guns.

While waiting for the order to advance, I lay on the soft green turf beside my horse transport company and watched the huge masses of the enemy slowly winding up the heights beyond the river and moving off to the north. Over their heads appeared in quick succession the fleecy white clouds caused by the bursts of our shrapnel and howitzer shells.

About 11 a.m. the order to move on arrived, and we descended the long winding road into the valley of the Marne. We halted at the foot of the hills about 1000 yards from the river, the horse transport parked in the fields on the right of the road, the artillery on the left; the infantry pressed on, crossed the river by the bridge, and scaled the opposite heights.

From our position with the Transport Train we could see in front of us the town of Nanteuil-sur-Marne nestling under the hills on the north bank of the river, while above it, on the ridge, our infantry were being shelled by the enemy's heavy artillery. Enormous black clouds of smoke, dust, and debris rose every time that one of these large shells struck the ground. Presently the enemy lengthened his range, and these huge shells began to fall nearer and nearer the train, till one exploded less than 100 yards away. The next we expected would alight in our midst, hurling men, horses, and waggons in fragments into the air, but fortunately the gunners again altered their range and shelled the ridge in our front.

The delay in our advance on the 9th between noon and 6 in the evening was difficult for us in the train to understand. The Germans, we were told, were in desperate plight this day, and if we could have pressed on, many thousands of exhausted men and much munitions of war might have fallen into our hands.

Conjectures were of course rife,—the French on our right and left were perhaps not able to advance, or possibly the British Divisions on our flanks were held up.

There may have been some cause for caution owing to the fact that the Germans had not destroyed a single bridge across the Marne. This may have been due to the hurried nature of their retreat, or it may have been that they hoped to resume the offensive shortly and would then require them, or perhaps the rapid advance of the allies frustrated any attempt at their destruction.

But there may have been a deep laid scheme to lure us beyond the river and then from the heights beyond hurl us into its blue depths.

At 6 p.m., however, the welcome order to advance was received, and we crossed the bridge into Nanteuil. A broken waggon of the Princess Victoria's 2nd Prussian Hussar Regiment lay in the street, and farther on other relics of the German flight were passed. Motor lorries, waggons, lances, rifles, boxes of ammunition and supplies, also articles of uniform, littered the road, but few dead or wounded did we see.

Night fell as we reached the heights north of Nanteuil, and we pushed on through the deserted village of Bèzu, till finally my company reached the brigade on outpost near Le Ventelet farm, about three miles north of Bèzu.

The general and his staff were asleep in a deep layer of straw at the foot of a rick, and a red lantern stuck on a post at their feet showed that this was Brigade Headquarters. Two of the battalions lay sleeping along the roadside, their rifles and accoutrements beside them, while the other two were scattered on outpost along the front, the artillery being near the Brigade Headquarters.

Waking young H——, the staff captain, I found out the position of the various units, and after distributing their supplies my company bivouacked on the edge of the wood near one of the battalions whose platoons lay sleeping on the ground in their ranks, looking in the pale moonlight like long rows of corpses laid out for burial.

No fires were permitted in this advanced position, and my men,

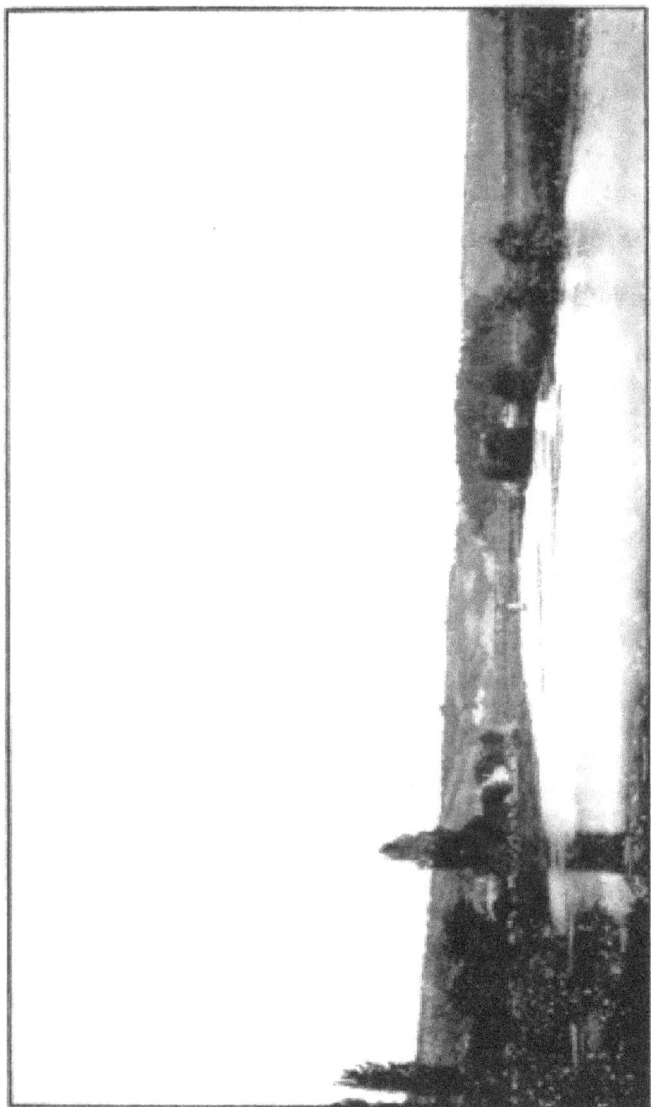

NANTEUIL-SUR-MARNE.

who had been up with the dawn of the previous day, now at 2 a.m., after twenty-one hours' consecutive work, lay down, utterly wearied, beside their horses for a couple of hours' rest.

At dawn on the 10th of September we were awakened by heavy artillery and rifle fire: another murderous day's work had begun. The staff, infantry, and gunners rose and went forward to the attack, and in a few minutes had disappeared into the raw morning mists, leaving us the sole occupants of the bivouac.

While fires were lit and men and horses fed I strolled over the ground. Soft grey red-banded caps, a few black leather spiked helmets, clips of mauser ammunition, a sword or two, a few dead horses, scraps of food, dirty paper, soiled pieces of uniform, and the charred remains of many fires, testified to the German occupation of this bivouac before our troops had reached it.

About 8 a.m. I had orders to return to Bèzu with the company to load supplies from the motor vehicles of the supply column. While proceeding with this work an ambulance drove up, and from its interior was gently removed the body of an officer of the Lincolns who had been killed the previous afternoon. It was reverently carried from the vehicle and placed on the altar steps of the little church of Bèzu, until fitting arrangements for burial could be made.

Later on, when the waggons had completed loading and I was waiting for the order to advance, I went in and sat down for a short rest in this little church. It had been used as a temporary hospital: straw and bloody bandages strewed the floor, and I sat there and reflected upon all the pain and suffering that war brings in its train. My silent companion lying so still at the far end upon the altar steps sent my thoughts to Old England, and I could see the sorrow and anguish that must be borne in many a home as the news arrived of the death of husband, brother, or son.

Presently a soldier tiptoed into the church, placed a canteen of tea beside my chair, and as silently left the building. This man passing outside had evidently noticed me sitting in the porch; perhaps he thought I looked tired or needed some refreshment, and, unbidden, brought me this tea. A kindly thought, a small unselfish act, but it teaches that war has a bright side. It may bring forth all man's primeval passions, but it also brings forth many grand qualities—courage, self-sacrifice, a great unselfishness, chivalry, and a high sense of duty.

At last the welcome order to move on arrived, and we proceeded by the road winding over the hill north of Bèzu. Presently we passed

GERMAN WAGON.

a wood, and behind the trees lay what had been yesterday a Prussian battery. Today the guns remained silent, while stretched upon the earth around lay the bodies of those who had served them.

It had been just an episode common enough in war. The guns belching forth fire and death, the gunners intent on their murderous work, while through the wood come stealing unseen the British infantry. Suddenly a terrific burst of rifle fire, and one gun and then another becomes silent, till at last all is over, the gunners lie dead, and the guns are the trophies of the victors.

In the afternoon I left the train and went on in the car to join my brigade, taking S———, my subaltern, who was driving. To avoid having to pass columns of infantry plodding along the road we turned off on to a side road running through the woods. The sounds of artillery and rifle fire grew louder as we left the main body and caught up with the advance-guard.

Presently we passed some dead Germans lying by the roadside; the tide of battle had surged on and left them unheeded where they fell.

Suddenly the car rounded a corner, and to my amazement we found ourselves confronted by three of the enemy standing in a bunch at the side of the road. No other troops, either British or German, were in sight at the moment, and I concluded that these had avoided our advance-guard and were now attempting to escape through the woods. The car was pulled up, and leaping from it, I ran towards the group, shouting to them to put their hands up while I covered them with my revolver. As I approached they moved apart, disclosing a fourth enemy seated on the ground having a wounded limb dressed by a British chaplain. The latter now looked up with a smile, saying, "You can put away that gun, these men have already surrendered."

"Yes, we have surrendered," repeated one of the prisoners in excellent English. So, much to my regret, I was forestalled from leading three stalwart prisoners into our lines, but the manner in which my hopes had been dashed to the ground caused me much subsequent amusement.

I now noticed that these men had no rifles, but retained their side-arms and ammunition pouches. They were Bavarians, well set up, clean, smart-looking men.

The chaplain having finished dressing the fourth prisoner's wound, suggested that I should take the man to the nearest field dressing-station. To this I agreed, and he was placed in the car.

At this time the British Army was unaware of the awful atrocities being then perpetrated by these same Germans in unhappy Belgium, atrocities which for bloodlust and savagery exceed the fiendish tortures of the middle ages. Had we but known of these, the chaplain, I think, would scarcely have shown so affectionate a regard for these outrageous ruffians.

Leaving our wounded prisoner at the dressing-station established in the next village, where many other wounded, both British and German, were now being brought, we pushed on to Chèzy, which we reached about 4 p.m. Here in the church and outside it were congregated a mass of German prisoners guarded by a few of our soldiers. These Germans were mostly infantrymen—big, fine looking fellows. They had had neither rest nor food, however, for nearly forty-eight hours, and seemed glad to be taken, especially as they were told they would be supplied with rations as soon as the supply section of the Horse Train arrived. Later in the evening I spoke to several, and found that many of them could speak excellent English, and had been in England in various civil occupations only a few weeks before. To my great astonishment my chauffeur, a native of Edinburgh, met one prisoner who had been a waiter at the North British Hotel in that city, and had been friends with him under very different circumstances from the present.

The pursuit of the German forces was continued until exhaustion and the fall of night put an end to it.

The Battle of the Marne was over, and what a triumph indeed for the Allies! The advance on Paris stopped; the invincible German armies hurled back across the river; many thousands of the enemy killed and wounded, and many thousands more taken prisoners.

THE CHURCH AT BÈZU.

CHAPTER 6

The Pursuit to the Aisne

My company of the train handed over one day's rations to the troops at Dammard, and then returned to Chèzy to load one day's iron rations—*i.e.,* preserved meat, biscuits, tea, sugar, and Oxo cubes packed in canisters.

Every soldier is normally supposed to carry one iron ration in his haversack, which is never to be eaten except in emergency, and even then only on the direct order of an officer. The ordinary ration suffices for the day's needs, and is a very liberal one, consisting of meat, bread, bacon, jam, cheese, sugar, tea, salt, pepper, and mustard. There are occasions, however, when it is not possible to hand over this ration to the troops; the march may be so long that the men have completely outdistanced the vehicles containing their food, or the troops may be under such close fire that it would be impossible to bring the train waggons up to them.

It is to meet such contingencies as these that the iron ration is provided.

It had been eaten by my division at the Battle of Mons, and this was the first opportunity afforded us of replacing it.

The train waggons arrived at Chèzy about midnight on the 11th, and met the motor vehicles of the supply column in the square opposite the church. Here the transference of the loads was made, the supply column returned to railhead many miles to the south, while my company of the train proceeded back to Dammard, where it arrived about 3 a.m. on the 12th.

At 6 a.m. I was awakened, and crawled from under a waggon feeling stiff, sore, and ill from lack of sufficient sleep.

As I struggled to my feet, however, and slowly opened my eyes, all my weariness was instantly forgotten in the wonderful picture that

GERMAN PRISONERS TAKEN AFTER THE BATTLE OF THE MARNE.

struck my astonished gaze.

It had been raining during the night, and there before me, on the bare sodden hill-top, showing up plainly against the dark background of clouds, were great masses of French cavalry. The squadrons were halted, and except for the occasional toss of a horse's head or the flick of a tail there was not a movement in all those serried ranks.

The attention of both men and horses seemed to be riveted upon the dark valley at their feet and the bare slopes of the open hillsides beyond.

It was not the numbers of the troops nor their attitude of concentrated attention that left me breathless with amazement, but the fact that these soldiers had brought into a modern battlefield the brilliant costumes and bright panoply of war associated with a bygone age.

Nearest to me were *cuirassiers* and dragoons, big men on heavy horses dressed in dark-blue tunics and steel breastplates, baggy scarlet breeches and long jack-boots, while on their heads were brass or steel helmets, from which drooped long crimson horsehair plumes. Farther on were other regiments, evidently hussars, smaller men on lighter horses, in sky-blue silver-buttoned jackets and caps, and bright red breeches.

I rubbed my eyes and pinched myself, was I really awake, or was I not dreaming of one of Meissonier's famous pictures? My tired brain was assuredly conjuring up a vision ninety nine years old of an episode in that campaign which I had studied so carefully some years before for my promotion examination.

These men nearest me must be Kellermann's heavy cavalry, and those beyond the light horsemen of Lefèbre-Desnouettes. Watch!— these squadrons will suddenly break into frenzied excitement, swords will leap into the air, the horsemen rise in their stirrups, and a roar of "*Vive l'Empereur!*" will roll again and again down the long lines, while riding slowly across the front will come that familiar figure bunched up awkwardly on a beautiful white horse—the figure of the greatest soldier of all the ages. I think I can see him in his green *chasseur* jacket and white breeches, his head sunk forward on his breast, his right hand in the flap of his coat, while from under his plain cocked hat burn those deep set wonderful eyes, looking straight ahead, regardless of the adoration of his soldiers.

But no, this is 1914—not 1815; my grimy hands, my mud-stained khaki uniform, and a great emptiness beneath my Sam Browne belt, bring me back with a jerk to my day's duty.

A word of command and the picturesque squadrons ride forward down the slope, while I turn and join my own company, now filing out into the road.

Later on the rain came down in torrents, turning the wheel-scarred roads into deep lanes of mud, and greatly impeding our pursuit of the beaten enemy.

Through Roset-St-Albins and Oulchy-la-Ville the advance continued to Grand-Rozoy, where late in the afternoon a halt was called.

A broken down and deserted German convoy was found on the main Soissons road a couple of miles farther on, from which we obtained some supplies and forage.

As usual, the Army Service Corps seemed to work all night as well as march all day. It was not until daylight on the 12th that the train waggons were loaded from the Supply Column, horses and men having obtained a very short rest in the cold and wet by the roadside.

From the high ground near Cuiry-Housse we caught our first glimpse of the valley of the Aisne and the heights beyond it, which were to become later the scene of such titanic and prolonged fighting.

The British Cavalry Corps which was out in our front gradually drove the enemy before them, and about 4 in the afternoon my division commenced the long winding descent into the little town of Braine.

Halfway down the road I stopped, and turning to my left examined the magnificent view before me.

The flat level valley of the Aisne between Soissons and Vailly was spread at my feet. In the foreground on the left, nestling round its church spire, was the little village of Augy; on the right were the outskirts of Braine, while beyond them, above the woods, rose the hill of Brenelle, where our guns were subsequently placed. At the foot of Brenelle among the trees lay the village of Chassemy, which was being shelled, and as I looked a high-explosive shell set fire to some of the houses and a great column of white smoke blew away to the right over Brenelle.

On the horizon straight ahead, stretching to right and left, were the heights above the river, the Aisne itself being hidden by the intervening ground.

Continuing on my way I entered Braine, where heavy street fighting had taken place earlier in the day. Just outside the town the adventurous Bertrand Stewart had been killed, but not until his rifle had sent several Germans to their last account. Poor Bertrand Stewart, how he must have suffered at the Prussian hands during his imprisonment as a spy, for his hatred of the race was intense. He was a brave man and died the death he sought, seeking vengeance on his enemies.

My brigade spent the night of the 12th at Brenelle, and early on the 13th the attack on the enemy was resumed all along the line. On our left was the 5th Division, on our right the 1st, 2nd, and 4th Divisions; beyond them on each side the French prolonged the line.

By the evening the enemy had been thrown across the river with the loss of several of his big guns, and our own people had a footing on the northern bank, although all the bridges across the river had been destroyed.

The whole stretch of road between Braine and the Aisne through Chassemy had been under the enemy's heavy shell fire all day. Our Divisional Headquarters had sheltered just off the road behind a haystack.

The general's kitchen waggon, which was on the road, had been struck by a shell, and the waggon, horses, and driver, with all the pots and pans, had been blown to fragments.

At 4 in the afternoon the train waggons were loaded with supplies from the Motor Supply Column in the square of Braine, and at 7.30 p.m., just as dusk was settling down, all the horse-drawn vehicles of the train pulled out of the town and commenced their march over the shell-strewn road through Chassemy to the Aisne.

During the day this road was impassable: it stretched, a narrow white ribbon, across the level open valley in full view of the German gunners, who from their positions on the heights across the river could drop their shells on every yard of it. The friendly covering of night alone rendered it somewhat less dangerous.

About 10 p.m. we reached Chassemy. It was pitch dark. The heavy firing of the day had ceased, and only occasionally a flash and the deep rumble of a distant gun came down to one like the muttering of a summer night's thunderstorm on the far horizon.

The ugly form of a dead horse, which had been dragged to the roadside, was just discernible in the darkness at frequent intervals.

In the village of Chassemy the silence of death reigned: no troops were in this shell trap, and the inhabitants had fled. Every living creature had been terrified by the bursting shells and the falling masonry, for I could see neither flesh nor fowl in the place. Some of the houses were in ruins, in others huge holes had been made; some had caught

BRAINE.

fire but had now burned out, and only the dull glow and smell of burning remained.

The clattering of the horses' hoofs over the silent cobble streets seemed to me an inferno of noise that would bring every German shell for miles around bursting round our ears.

Beyond Chassemy the road ran through a dense wood for about a mile, near the farther end of which, on the right-hand side, we came to the white wooden gates of the *château* of Chassemy. Here was General Gough's headquarters on this night.

At the gates stood the quartermasters of the various regiments waiting to guide us to the river banks half a mile farther on, where fatigue parties would carry the supplies on their backs the remaining distance. Not a light of any kind was allowed, nor was smoking or talking permitted, and after a short whispered conversation the march to the river bank was continued.

The Germans knew that supplies of food and ammunition could only reach our infantry by this road, which led across the Aisne over Vailly bridge, now destroyed, to the little town of the same name on the northern bank.

The bridge-head was only 2500 yards from the German gun position on the heights of Condé, and from this vantage-point the gunners rained their shrapnel and high explosive on the approaches. By day no creature could live beneath that hail of lead and jagged steel, and it was only under cover of night that it was possible to transfer the soldiers' needs to the northern bank.

From the edge of the wood the road ran for 600 yards to the bridge-head over absolutely open country, without a vestige of cover. This stretch of ground was now littered with dead horses, and it was difficult in the extreme to get the waggons past the poor fallen beasts, who had been left as they fell, some in the middle of the road.

On arrival at the bridge-head the supplies were taken off the waggons as rapidly as possible and carried by the ration parties through Vailly to the hastily-dug trenches above the town.

The bridge across the Aisne had been blown up by the enemy, but the stone buttresses remained standing, and across these planks had been laid. These formed the sole communication between our infantry, hanging on desperately to their hard-won positions on the north bank, and the remainder of the division on the south bank.

Across this narrow unstable bridge I walked, the planks bending beneath my weight. In front of me was Vailly, dark and silent as the grave; above me the hill on which British and Prussians faced each other only a few yards apart, and upon which they were now hastily digging themselves into mother earth, so that when daylight came they would have secured some measure of shelter from the screeching shells and deadly bullets. Below me flowed the dark waters of the river, while up-stream on my right some sapper companies were constructing a pontoon bridge.

Suddenly, as the ration party and I were proceeding through the deserted streets of Vailly, past the demolished cottages and battered houses, hell burst above our heads. Thousands of rifles were fired, sending their death-dealing missiles through the night as fast as the soldiers could pull the bolts and press the triggers; guns too joined in, the blinding flashes and terrific thunderclaps of the bursting shells adding to the fearful uproar.

We knew what was happening. The Germans were making a counter-attack, hurling great masses of men against our thin devoted khaki line.

There was nothing for us to do but wait until the attack was over. Leaving the road we sought the cover of a deserted factory, and under its friendly walls we sheltered from the flying bullets and screaming shells.

Every round from a German rifle or gun that missed the parapet above seemed to come shrieking with rage into the streets of Vailly or to the bridge-head on the river bank.

What were our thoughts during these moments? We knew that in the hell and darkness above us hundreds of human souls were swiftly passing into the Great Beyond, thousands of our fellow beings were struggling for mastery on that hilltop. And who would be successful— the dense masses of the Prussians, whose shouts we could hear amid the tumult, or our own staunch hearted brethren? The courage of our men we never doubted, but they were so few, and there were no reserves,—every rifle was in the firing line. If that thin line broke there was nothing in front of the Prussians but the ration party waiting quietly amid the sacks of bread and the cases of jam and meat.

The same indomitable spirit, however, that clung to the bloody heights of Albuera, that swept the French waves of cavalry from Waterloo and the hosts of Russian infantry from the hill of Inkerman, now shattered the dense masses of the *Kaiser's* choicest troops.

The counter-attack was beaten off, the rifles ceased their dreadful crackle, the guns paused in their murderous work, and the attenuated band of British soldiers, their weapons almost red-hot in their hands, now obtained a short respite to recover breath.

The ration parties picked up their loads and ascended the hill.

Presently we met a stream of men making their way painfully along. These were the wounded. Some, with bandaged heads or arms, were walking unassisted; others were being carried pick-a-back by their unwounded comrades, while others were lying still and pale, borne upon stretchers.

What agony some of these men must be suffering, yet not a groan, not a murmur of complaint did I hear! Brave, noble fellows!

At last I found Brigade Headquarters in a small house in the main street. The general had just turned in to snatch a few hours' sleep, but I saw young H——, the staff captain, a gallant boy, the sight of whose cheery smile and amusing swagger was the finest of tonics at the end of a long, hard, depressing day.

Having made my report I returned to Braine, where I arrived at 3 a.m. on the 14th with my company.

The German retreat I felt was over, at any rate for the present, and the enemy was now entrenching himself in a previously selected and naturally strong defensive position.

British wounded being evacuated from Braine.

CHAPTER 7

Operations on the Aisne

Now begins that stage of the war which can best be described as a
siege,—a siege, not of a walled fortress whose defences can be carried
by assault, but the siege of two great nations, whose frontiers extend
beyond the range of vision of the combatants.

The defences themselves seem so insignificant: not great, thick,
towering walls and castellated turrets, with the defenders plainly visible keeping watch and ward on the ramparts, but a long low mound
of earth, thrown from a trench, stretching in an irregular wavy line to
right and left over hill and dale as far as the eye can reach.

Running approximately parallel to this long mound of earth is
another one, and in the trench behind it you will find the Allied Armies.

That portion of this trench which is occupied by the British runs
roughly from Condé on the left to Meulins on the right, along the
high ground of the northern bank of the Aisne.

My own division, the 3rd, was entrenched on the outskirts of Vailly,
and from their position our infantry could see to the north, 300 yards
away, the German trenches; to the south the river flowed at their backs,
while farther south, beyond the river, was the high ground of Brenelle,
where our artillery was placed in support. Across the open intervening plain ran the white road through Chassemy to Braine in full view
of friend and foe. On this road during daylight no living creature was
ever to be seen, but during the hours of darkness it teemed with life.

On the outward journey came full convoys of food and ammunition, picks and shovels, reinforcements of men and empty ambulance
waggons, while on the homeward journey travelled empty convoys
and full ambulances containing maimed and suffering humanity.

On the 14th September the Germans shelled our positions so severely that one of our batteries of artillery was forced to leave its guns until they could be recovered under the shadow of night. Some of our cavalry, too, which had been hanging on to a very exposed position on the north bank of the river, were obliged to withdraw, and as the day lengthened it became more and more obvious that the German position was immensely strong, and that the enemy was present in such great numbers that we should be sore put to it to hold our own against his violent and repeated attacks.

On this night my subaltern took the supply waggons out to Vailly, enabling me to obtain a good night's rest—the first I had enjoyed since I slept at Meaux a fortnight before.

On the 15th, Divisional Headquarters took up their abode in a little country house just out of Braine, while in the town were billeted the Train and the Field Ambulances. The horses were picketed in the streets tied to trees, the vehicles pulled on to the pavements.

During the morning as many of the wounded as were fit to travel were brought out of the temporary hospital, established in a large empty house in the church square; they were then gently lifted in the stretchers upon which they were lying, and placed in motor-lorries on a deep layer of straw. As each lorry was filled it was driven to the station, where an ambulance train was in waiting to take the patients to a base port for transmission to England.

On this day there were over 160 sent away. Some were dreadfully hurt, many were suffering from head wounds, and one poor fellow had half his face torn away by a fragment of shell.

Though every case which could be evacuated safely was despatched to the base, yet daily the numbers of wounded increased, till not only the temporary hospital but the big church in the square was filled.

The German wounded in our hands were kept in a separate building, attended to by one of their own doctors, and supplied with the same comforts and medical necessaries as our own people.

In the evening I marched out with my company to Vailly bridge. In the dusk, between Braine and Chassemy, we passed many newly made graves; some were in the open fields, others in woods or thickets beside the road. Most of these graves were lying singly, dug on the spot where the soldier had fallen; but at the junction of some cross-roads we came to a group of five, of which two were awaiting occupants. These yawning graves, reminders of the fate which might be in store for us at any moment, did not increase our cheerfulness, as can well be imagined.

By the time we reached Chassemy it was as black as the ace of spades and raining heavily.

Through the deserted, shot-ridden village, past the *château* gates, we came at last to the edge of the wood 400 yards from the bridge-head. Here in the deep shadow of the trees were drawn up the field ambulances waiting for their nightly loads of wounded.

Passing the Red Gross vehicles, which we could barely discern in the blackness, we came out into the open stretch of road leading off to the river banks. Over the dead horses still lying in the way we stumbled. Holding our noses as the awful stench of the putrefying carcasses struck our nostrils, we came at last to the plank bridge across the Aisne.

Here, in the pitchy darkness, the rain, and the horrid smells, we complete our work. The ration parties unload the waggons, jostling each other and tripping over the horrible obstructions in the road as they toil wearily between the waggons and the trenches. In the opposite direction comes a stream of dark figures moving slowly and painfully along. This procession is liberally besmirched with splashes of white, which alone shows up out of the darkness.

For this mournful procession we stand aside, and the tired soldiers with their heavy loads forbear to move, lest they should cause any further pain to this poor pitiful stream of humanity, swathed in bandages, as it makes its way to the shelter of the ambulances by the wood.

About 3.30 a.m. on the morning of the 16th I returned with my company to Braine, more than thankful that the enemy had refrained from shelling Vailly bridge and its approaches while we were there.

The hour of our arrival at Vailly was altered from time to time to circumvent the unwelcome attentions of the German gunners, who night after night drew their bows at a venture on to the river banks.

On the 16th and 17th the enemy made repeated attacks on our infantry, which were driven off, and engaged in artillery duels with our gunners, but met with little success.

On the 18th, as I was starting at dusk on the usual nightly visit to the Aisne, I saw the 6th Division, which had just arrived from home, come marching through Braine. How welcome was this reinforcement to our sorely tried little army! With the new division was my brother, and it was good to squeeze his hand and exchange a word of greeting as he passed with his battalion *en route* to Soupir.

On the 19th the transport companies started out about an hour later than usual on their trip to Vailly. Riding along with me was an old friend whom I had served with in South Africa, Captain S——, of an Irish regiment. We talked of the old days on the *veldt*, and discussed the present murderous war.

My friend had a presentiment that he was shortly to be killed. I endeavoured to turn his thoughts to a more cheerful subject, but did not attempt to pooh-pooh the idea as a fantasy of the brain caused through physical depression, as such presentiments are common among soldiers and unfortunately are usually confirmed.

It was a starlight night, the moon had not yet risen, and we passed in the dark the objects on the road so familiar by now,—the same shell blown walls, the same dead horses and the same old smells,—till we came without adventure on to the open road near the river bank.

Suddenly a rifle shot broke out in the still darkness ahead, followed by a terrific roar of musketry. Another of the oft-repeated German attacks on our trenches was being made,—so often in the last few days had the enemy in overwhelming numbers tried to push our men into the river that flowed at their backs. On every occasion, however, had that wonderful British infantry repelled the attack and forced the Germans to draw back, leaving their dead and wounded in countless numbers strewing the narrow valley of death between the opposing trenches.

From our position the whole hill top reminded me of a grass fire seen flickering across the veldt on a South African night.

The German bullets that missed the hill now came flying amongst us and over our heads. The Prussian infantry when charging have a trick of shooting from the hip, with the result that the bullet flies high, and is therefore more dangerous to those some distance ahead than to those close in front.

The German artillery on the hill of Condé now joined in and shelled the bridge approaches where we were, in order to keep off any reinforcements we might be sending forward to our hard-pressed infantry.

Fortunately for us these shells were oversighted about a hundred yards, and the shrapnel, bursting with its blinding flash and sharp detonation, threw its leaden pellets some little distance to our right.

Under these most unpleasant conditions our work continued. The Army Service Corps soldier in his rather humdrum occupation has often to run the risks of his purely fighting brother of the line without participating in any of the glory or excitement which fall to the lot of the latter. The A.S.C. driver is shot at without the satisfaction of being able to shoot back, but he carries on his work with the most extraordinary coolness and phlegm, often under the most trying conditions. It is only when his horses are hit that he displays any sign of excitement, for he is, as a rule, devoted to the animals placed in his charge.

Suddenly a star-shell bursts right above us, throwing its brilliant light over the working parties, over the plank bridge, and the now completed pontoon bridge higher upstream, and over all the approaches to the river on both banks.

This bright illumination only lasts a few seconds, and after its blinding glare the night seems blacker than ever.

The uproar gradually lessens, and finally dies down to a spasmodic burst or two and a few individual rifle shots.

The German bugles are now plainly heard, but whether sounding the rally or a fresh charge it is impossible to say: if the latter it does not materialise, for the night from now onwards is quiet except for a sniper at work, or the occasional shot of some soldier whose nerves will not allow him to rest, and amid the dark forms stretched on the ground in front of his trench he sees a phantom figure creeping forward to grip him by the throat.

What the casualties are in front we do not know, but we ourselves have not escaped scathless. One man has been shot in the spine as he stooped over a sack of oats, another poor fellow must have been hit in the head by a piece of flying shrapnel as he crossed the plank bridge, for he and his load disappeared with a dull splash into the river below and were no more seen.

As for my poor friend S——, his disappearance on this night has been an unsolved mystery. From the time we arrived at the bridgehead he was never seen again. Perhaps he too was hit as he crossed the river, and the dark waters of the Aisne closing over him have hid him from sight. He was officially returned as "missing."

Crossing to Vailly I went to report to Brigade Headquarters. What a horrid sight the little town presented. Great heaps of fallen masonry and charred woodwork showed where once a well-built house had stood; farther on were a row of roofless villas, with great gaping holes in their walls; while down by the river bank was a terrace of little cottages, of which only the smoke blackened outside walls now remained. The streets were littered with stone and bricks, slates and fragments of glass, overturned vehicles and dead horses. The whole atmosphere was tainted with the odour of burning and the disgusting smell of putrefying flesh.

Nearly all the inhabitants of Vailly had left before the British occupation, but one or two people still remained,—some because, poor creatures! they had nowhere else to go. One such unfortunate family of father, mother, and five children, very poor peasants, occupied a little cottage by the river bank. Here they huddled together during the frequent bombardments, praying, I have no doubt, to their God, the All Mighty and the All Merciful, to protect them. A German shell entered that cottage on this night, and when the dust and debris of the explosion had cleared away there was but the mother with one child left alive. What had the other poor innocent little children done that they should have met so terrible a fate?

I had some difficulty in finding Brigade Headquarters, as they had moved since my last visit, and were now occupying a large barn, of which half the roof was missing. The general greeted me in his usual kindly manner, but he and his staff were grave and anxious; the losses had been very severe during the strenuous fighting of the last few days, and reinforcements were badly needed. Fortunately these were now arriving; not only had I seen the 6th Division, but fresh drafts for the depleted regiments were also hourly expected.

On the 20th September, thanks to the timely arrival of the 6th Division, it was possible to relieve some of the troops who had been in the trenches now continuously for a week, and were showing signs of exhaustion. Two of the battalions of my brigade were consequently withdrawn on this night, 20th-21st September, other troops taking their places.

On the following night, 21st-22nd September, the other two battalions were likewise withdrawn, and the whole brigade was concentrated at Courçelles by the morning of the 22nd.

Here officers and men enjoyed four days' complete rest. Considering the terrible time they had been through in the trenches, it was wonderful how cheerful they all were; their morale was certainly not impaired.

About this time, too, the horse transport companies of the Train which had been billeted in Braine were ordered out of the town, and with some artillery and other mounted units bivouacked in the fields between Braine and Courçelles. Here the men built themselves some very comfortable straw and brushwood shelters covered with waterproof sheets or sacking.

On the Courçelles road we daily carried out the loading of the Supply waggons.

On the night of the 26th September the brigade moved out again to its former position on the outskirts of Vailly, relieving another brigade in the trenches. The smells on the road were now much less disagreeable, as the dead horses had been removed.

The fatigue parties engaged on the unpleasant task of burying these carcasses found the body of a soldier of the Royal Scots Greys lying beside his horse. How long, we wondered, had this poor fellow been lying there. Night after night we must have passed him by, unconscious of his presence.

On the 29th September I took a car and drove out to Meulins, on the extreme right of the British position, to see my brother, whose regiment had suffered very heavily during a German attack a few days previously.

On the way I had to cross one or two streams, the bridges over which had been blown up by the enemy during his retreat to the Aisne. Communication between the banks had been restored by trestle or pontoon bridges built by the R..E.

On reaching Bourg I found that this little town had been shelled by the German 11-inch howitzers, and complete buildings had been utterly demolished by the giant missiles fired from this weapon. These shells were commonly known among the troops as "Black Marias," owing to the huge black clouds of smoke, earth, rock, and debris thrown into the air by the explosion of the shell on impact.

Most of the wretched inhabitants were living in cellars, where they fondly imagined themselves safe.

Between Bourg and Meulins I passed several "Black Maria" holes which resembled miniature craters, and were big enough to have buried twenty men.

In areas where the shelling had been frequent, "funk holes" or bomb proof shelters had been made, into which those in the vicinity had rushed for cover when they heard one of these big shells coming along. It was curious to see in many places how closely the shells had fallen to these shelters.

These "funk holes" were only safe as a protection against the flying pieces of metal and debris caused by the explosion. A direct hit would have pierced the timber baulks and thick layer of earth covering the bomb-proof, and, exploding within, would have blown the unfortunate occupants in pieces into the air.

Near Meulins one of our batteries of artillery was hidden in a little thicket, and so well concealed from the enemy's aeroplanes that

STAFF OF THE 9TH BRIGADE AT COURÇELLES.

every effort of the German gunners to locate the battery had failed. Their attempts, however, to destroy the guns were plainly visible in a ploughed field fifty to a hundred yards away, which was pitted so closely all over with shell holes as to resemble the face of a man who had had smallpox.

On the high ground about two miles north-east of Meulins I found the West Yorkshire Regiment on the extreme right of our line. Beyond them was a battalion of baggy-trousered picturesque Turcos.

My brother's company was in support of the fire trenches in a series of pits outside which the men lay to fire when repelling an infantry assault, but within which they crawled and took shelter during an artillery bombardment.

Officers and men seemed very cheerful, in spite of the fearful experiences which they had been through, having lost fifty *per cent* of their numbers within a week of their arrival on the Aisne.

The British regimental officer and Private Thomas Atkins are splendid fellows, and for them I have the most profound admiration. Their magnificent courage, readiness of resource in trying situations, powers of endurance, marvellous patience, and never-failing cheerfulness under the most depressing circumstances, render them fighting men without equal in all the world.

On the night of 1st October two battalions of my brigade—the Royal Scots Fusiliers and Northumberland Fusiliers—were withdrawn from Vailly and brought back into billets at Augy, and on this night a few of us were told that our division would leave the Aisne and our portion of the line would be taken over by the French.

This scheme, as a matter of fact, embraced the whole British Army, which was to move to Flanders; but so well was the secret kept that we had no idea that other divisions beyond our own were being withdrawn, nor had we the smallest inkling of our destination.

Rumours and conjectures were of course numerous, in which even Calais and a return to England figured.

On the night of the 2nd, two other battalions were also withdrawn, and by the morning of the 3rd the whole brigade was concentrated at Cramaille and Saponay. On this day, too, I left the brigade with deep regret to take over a more responsible appointment attached to the staff of the division.

What the feelings of the rest of the army were on our departure from the Aisne I cannot say, but personally I heaved a deep sigh of relief when I turned my back on that river.

The memory of Vailly will be indelibly stamped on my brain as a hideous nightmare of noisome odours, screaming shells, burning shot-ridden buildings, dark streets littered with fragments of houses, dead horses and overturned vehicles, and a continuous stream of broken, bandage-swathed men toiling wearily across the plank bridge over the dark waters of the Aisne.

"BLACK MARIA" HOLES AND BOMB-PROOF SHELTER.

CHAPTER 8

The Move to Flanders

Every possible precaution was taken to keep the withdrawal of the British from the Aisne and their subsequent movements concealed from the enemy. The troops handed their trenches over during the night to the French, and all marches were made in the hours of darkness, while by day, men, horses, and guns were hidden in woods and villages.

I left Braine about 11 p.m. on the 2nd October, reaching Beugneux about 1 a.m. on the morning of the 3rd, where I spent the rest of the night sleeping on the floor in a farmhouse.

The movements of the troops on this night were somewhat hindered by a thick fog, which served, however, as an additional screen to the withdrawal. In the early hours of the morning the 9th Brigade arrived at Cramaille and Saponay, the 7th at Noroy, and the 8th at Troesnes.

At sunset the march was continued to Marolles and La Ferté-Milon, where Divisional Headquarters were temporarily accommodated in a beautiful French *château*.

On the afternoon of the 4th the scheme for entraining the troops on the following day was explained by the staff, and in the evening I was despatched in a car to Fère-en-Tardenois, which was Sir John French's headquarters at this time, to obtain further details regarding supply arrangements.

On my return to La Ferté-Milon about 10 p.m. I found the last of the troops departing. I therefore went on to Crépy en Valois, which I reached about 1 a.m., and joined some of the staff seated at supper in a country house on the outskirts of the town.

At 5 a.m. on the morning of the 5th we were all up once more. A very busy day lay before us. The whole Division of 17,000 men and

6000 horses was to entrain from four stations—Compiègne, Le Meux, Longueil-Ste-Marie, and Pont-Ste-Maxence.

The first and last places were about fifteen miles apart, with Le Meux and Longueil-Ste-Marie close together about midway between the two.

Various officers were detailed to make the necessary arrangements at each station. One supply officer was detailed to Compiègne, another to Pont-Ste-Maxence, while I looked after the other two places.

From each of the four stations a train correctly composed of the requisite number of passenger coaches, horse boxes, and open trucks for guns and vehicles was to leave every four hours without intermission until the whole division had been despatched.

The preliminary arrangements had to be carefully made out in great detail. Each unit required a certain amount of time to entrain, as horses had to be boxed and guns run on to the trucks. Mounted units took longer than others. As each train left the station a fresh lot of troops were timed to arrive, but at no station had there to be more troops than the next train could deal with.

Time-tables were accordingly prepared and issued to all concerned.

Passing through Verberie I crossed the splendid bridge of barges built by the French engineers over the Oise to replace the stone structure which had been destroyed during the retreat, arriving at Le Meux about 8 a.m.

Here I arranged with the mayor for the supply and distribution to the troops of wood, straw, and hay, then proceeded to Longueil-Ste-Marie, where I made similar arrangements. Later on I visited Pont-Ste-Maxence and Compiègne, passing at the latter place the remains of the fine stone bridge destroyed by the French to check the Prussian pursuit in August. At these two places I found all supply arrangements satisfactorily completed, and my two officers busy assisting in entraining the troops.

Everywhere I found the French authorities most helpful and sympathetic, assisting the troops in every possible manner. In this, the greatest democratic country in the world, the organisation for war and the patriotism and unselfishness of all classes of the people are beyond praise. Every able-bodied man must defend his country, his home, and his womenkind; if not willingly, then by compulsion.

We in England consider it necessary to appeal through brightly coloured posters to the youths who leave others to save their homes from the flames, their women from outrage, and their business from ruin.

In democratic France every man and woman must bear their share of the nation's sufferings. Those men who are not shouldering the rifle are mobilised and working in factories for the Army's needs as soldiers at soldiers' wages.

The first trains filled with troops left the four stations during the forenoon, and as they steamed out the head of the next column to entrain marched into the yards. With wonderful regularity the work continued, train after train departing at fourhour intervals.

Still no one knew our destination.

Through the night of the 5th and all the next day the troops arrived, entrained, and passed on. By 9 p.m. on the 6th the last of our division had gone.

Motor cars now collected those officers whose work was completed, and about 10 p.m. we congregated at Verberie, where' several of the staff of the division had also assembled, though the general and his personal staff had left on the previous day.

After some supper we started off in six cars, only the officer in the leading car knowing the destination or route.

After a dusty and very weary journey, travelling all night and proceeding *via* Beauvais and Poix, at each of which places we stopped half an hour, we arrived at Abbeville at 6 a.m. on the 7th.

Here, at the Hotel Tête de Boeuf, we met the general and the rest of the staff. Some of the troops had already arrived.

By the evening of the 8th the whole division was detrained and billeted in and about the villages of Le Boisle, Tollent-Rave, and Regnauville, and here we waited two days for the 5th Division to detrain and join up on our right.

On the evening of the 10th orders were received to march towards the north.

The Germans, having failed to reach Paris, were now endeavouring to secure Calais as a stepping-stone towards their great goal, London, the heart of the British Empire.

The artillery and other mounted troops pushed on through the night to Pernes *via* Brailly. The infantry were taken up by French motor buses, which went forward through Hesdin to Pernes and Tandry, returning empty *via* St Pol to pick up a fresh load of men.

By daylight on the morning of the 11th the whole division, very tired and dusty, was assembled in its new locality.

There was little time for rest, however, as an aeroplane had just alighted in the level country north of Pernes bringing information that German cavalry were a few miles in front of us. Forward, therefore, is the word once more, and at 9 a.m. the march is continued, our troops coming into contact with enemy patrols soon after and driving them before them.

We now come out upon a country absolutely different from anything we have yet seen. It is perfectly flat, there is not a hill of any kind to relieve the dull monotony of the level plain. Range of vision, however, is extraordinarily restricted owing to the close intersection of the country in every direction by hedges and rows of trees. The land, too, is thickly cultivated and woody, the fields are small and surrounded by thickset hedges. The big main *pavé* roads are fine wide thoroughfares running perfectly straight for miles, bordered on each side by lofty elms or graceful poplars. The country roads are very narrow, with soft surfaces, bounded on each side by broad, deep, rush grown dykes filled with black stagnant water. On the edge of the dykes grow willows, which, leaning over the water, assist in restricting the view.

In such low lying country drainage is very difficult, and water is reached a very few feet below the surface. Though many of the people speak French, especially those resident in the towns, the language of the country is Flemish. This brings home the fact that we are now in that portion of Europe which has been a battle-ground for centuries. Between here and the Zuyder Zee Spaniards and Dutchmen, French, English, and Germans, have struggled in turn for supremacy.

This is indeed the cockpit of Europe.

Such close flat country imposes its own restrictions upon modern methods of warfare.

The training manuals tell us that the long-range rifle of today requires a good field of view in order to obtain its maximum effectiveness. With the Mauser or Lee-Enfield the enemy can be destroyed while he is yet a thousand yards and more away. In this country, however, the field of view is limited to 600 yards or less. Both sides can therefore approach each other unseen, and the long-range power of the modern rifle becomes to a great extent a useless asset. A handy quick shooting weapon is, however, imperative to check the enemy as he covers the intervening space between the trenches in one swift rush. Here the short British rifle has a decided advantage over the longer, clumsier, but perhaps more accurate Mauser. Still greater under such conditions is the power of the machine-gun.

This deadly little weapon in its concealed and well-protected shelter, spitting out its stream of death at 600 rounds a minute, gives to one cool brave man the power of a thousand rifles. This is the weapon which the Germans possess in such great numbers and use so effectively.

With the artillery, the shooting must be by indirect fire—that is to say, the gunner cannot see his target, but must rely for accuracy on the orders and reports which he receives from the observing officer ahead, to whom he is connected by telephone.

When the enemy makes his rush across the open upon the trenches the range must be picked up like lightning, the shells following with the swiftness of the thunderbolt.

Here the gun which excels is the wonderful "*soixante-quinze*" of our Allies, in whose brave and skilful hands this weapon becomes the queen of field-guns.

Thus, in this as in all other battlefields, each nation enjoys its own particular advantage; but after all is said and done, we must ever remember that it is the man and not the weapon who will ultimately emerge victorious, and by the man is meant not the soldier only, but the nation behind him.

The army is but the sword of a nation, and the people who must win are those who possess the will to conquer.

By the night of the 11th of October the division was approximately on the line of the La Bassée canal to the north of Hinges, L'Ecleme, and Busnes. Headquarters were in the empty *château* of Hinges, which stands on a slight eminence in the open plain.

From a gap between the trees in the park one can see to the southeast the town of Béthune, with its massive church tower dominating the landscape. Beyond Béthune, right away out of the blue horizon, emerges faintly the long ridge of Notre Dame de Lorette.

Upon the blood soaked, shell scarred summit of this ridge some of the most desperate fighting of the war took place a few months later.

The operations this day did not cease till long after night had fallen. In the darkness the narrow winding country roads were most difficult to follow, and more than one waggon of the train strayed off the road in the pitchy blackness, meeting disaster in the slime and filthy water of a deep dyke beside the way.

On the 12th the advance was again continued, good progress being made in spite of the resistance of the enemy, now reinforced by some battalions of Jägers, who were splendidly handled and put up a very fine fight against superior numbers.

The whole of our line now swung round to the right, and by the evening our division was facing almost due east from Locon to Fosse.

During the morning a large body of French cavalry, cuirassiers and dragoons, were sent up to cover our left flank, and great enthusiasm was displayed by the troops of both nations as we jointly pressed on against the common enemy.

The French heavy cavalry are fine-looking men, splendidly mounted, but unsuitably clothed in our opinion for modern warfare.

The Divisional Staff spent the night at Zelobes, sleeping in a barn on a layer of straw covered with their greatcoats. Those lying nearest the door complained of cold and insisted on having it closed, those at the farther end of the building found the atmosphere close and insisted upon having the door open.

Between the two we spent an uncomfortable and draughty night.

On the 13th we captured Vieille Chapelle and La Couture after heavy fighting. As soon as these villages were in our hands the Germans turned upon them their heavy artillery, directing their fire particularly on the churches, which in such flat country make excellent targets for ranging upon. They were also singled out for destruction on the plea that they were used as observation posts.

The church of Vieille Chapelle was totally destroyed, the bursting shells having set fire to the building, which was completely gutted. The roof, after burning some time, fell in with a crash, sending a thousand sparks flying upward and littering the floor with charred woodwork and a mass of debris.

The church of La Couture suffered less severely, most of the damage being caused by one shell, which, entering through the stained glass window at the head of the building, struck the upper portion of the altar, hurling it and the crucifix into a myriad fragments across the floor. The shrapnel then exploded within the edifice, scattering its leaden pellets and jagged steel casing in all directions, smashing lamps, brass candelabra, and stained glass, and covering the whole interior with a thick layer of dust.

Just beyond the church was a cottage, above which a shell had burst, stripping the whole of the tiles off one side of the roof

On the 14th the fighting was resumed as we pressed forward to Neuve Chapelle and the Richebourgs. Progress, however, was slow, as the enemy was hourly reinforced.

During the day we suffered the great misfortune of losing our

FRENCH HEAVY CAVALRY PASSING BRITISH ARTILLERY NEAR ZELOBES.

general—Hubert Hamilton. He was a leader who inspired confidence in his soldiers, and his death at this time was a serious blow to the British Army.

He was riding forward with his Staff when a shrapnel burst above their heads. He alone was struck, and fell from his horse, being instantly killed.

His body was taken to La Couture and buried in the churchyard there.

The burial took place after dark during a tremendous German counter-attack on our lines, and amid the scream of shells and the roar of musketry it was difficult to hear the chaplain as he recited the beautiful words of the burial service. The scene was extraordinarily impressive: the noise of the conflict, the vivid flashes of the bursting shells as they momentarily lighted the sky, and the silent figures round the grave, reminded me of those magnificent lines from "*The Burial of Sir John Moore*"—

We buried him darkly at dead of night,
The sods with our bayonets turning;
By the struggling moonbeam's misty light,
And the lantern dimly burning.

The death of General Hamilton cast a gloom over the whole division, and his fine soldierly character and able leadership were greatly missed during the dark days that followed.

There is little time, however, in war for mourning. One's heart may be full of sorrow, but strenuous deeds have to be done which occupy all one's mind and attention.

On the 15th and following days desperate fighting took place by day and night, the enemy stubbornly contesting every foot of ground and making frequent counter-attacks as we pushed him back through Croix Barbée, Richebourg-St-Vaast, Richebourg l'Avoué and Neuve Chapelle towards Aubers and Illies.

The Supply Train waggons were loaded daily some two or three miles behind the trenches, and taken forward to the troops under cover of night.

The German counter-attacks were frequent during the hours of darkness, and the companies of the train would go forward as far as La Couture, or even within a few yards of the trenches, only to be held up until the counter-attacks had spent their force. On these occasions the companies were halted under such cover as was available, behind

Damage to cottage at La Couture by shrapnel.

farm buildings or in the streets of a village, the drivers, dismounted, standing at their horse's heads, while absolute silence was maintained.

Such experiences were of nightly occurrence, and the scene never lacked a certain degree of grandeur.

Around stood the silent men and horses looking like dim shadows in the darkness; overhead were the whistling bullets and the occasional screech of a shell; ahead the noise of the battle and the lightninglike flashes of the cracking shrapnel; while through the trees the night sky was lit in more than one place by the crimson glare of a burning village.

The fighting on the 16th and 17th between Croix Barbée and Neuve Chapelle was particularly severe as we crossed the big main road running from Estaires to La Bassée. In the dusk near Neuve Chapelle I passed several dead Prussians, Uhlans by their uniforms; others had fallen near Croix Barbée, while one lay a huddled ugly corpse at the foot of the Rouge Croix, a giant red Calvary beside the road.

Near by was a barn which had been held by the enemy; its door and roof were splintered by a hundred bullets, while its floor was littered with bloodstained rags and torn disgusting fragments of German uniforms.

In the garden of a neighbouring cottage were several newly made graves, English and German lying side by side. Upon a picture postcard pinned with a safety-pin to the rough little wooden cross at the head of the graves I read the names of those who had given their lives nobly for their country's sake.

On the 18th October our further progress was stopped by the arrival of huge masses of the enemy's troops, including a powerful force of artillery. Our gallant infantry dug themselves into the ground, knowing they would be attacked by ever increasing numbers of the foe, and that they must hold out, whatever the cost, and bar the road to the sea.

Divisional Headquarters took up their abode at Neuve Chapelle, an insignificant little village which later was to become famous as the scene of furious battles, and here, too, I secured a billet in a little cottage near headquarters.

CHAPTER 9

Neuve Chapelle

The village of Neuve Chapelle is shaped rather like a two-pronged fork, the handle of which points at an angle towards the enemy's lines. Most of the houses lie on each side of the one short street forming the handle, and also for a short distance along the two streets forming the prongs. At the junction of these two streets there stood a large building which was occupied by Divisional Headquarters. Opposite, down a side-street, was the cure's house, next door to the church.

Along the road which formed the southern prong of the fork was a tiny cottage, the last building in the village, where I was billeted with one of the Divisional Staff officers. From the windows at the back I looked out on to the Bois de Biez, about half a mile away. In front of the cottage ran the main road for seven miles to Béthune through Richebourg l'Avoué and past Le Tourêt.

About halfway between Richebourg l'Avoué and Neuve Chapelle one crossed the big main thoroughfare running from Estaires to La Bassée. This road ran perfectly straight throughout its entire length, a magnificent tree-lined avenue standing several feet above the surrounding country. Dotted along the sides were cottages and farms, also little hamlets such as Pont Logy, Rouge Croix, and Pont-du-Hem. The southern end of this road for about one and a half miles from La Bassée was in the hands of the enemy, the remainder in our possession. Where this thoroughfare crossed the Neuve Chapelle Béthune road there stood an inn, which roughly marked the junction of our line with that of the 5th Division, which prolonged our front to the south.

This inn was for a time the headquarters of one of the infantry brigades of the 5th Division, and owing to its position at the junction of these important cross-roads it received a great deal of unwelcome attention from the German gunners. They plastered the vicinity at intervals with their shells, hoping to secure a hit on supplies, ammunition, or reinforcements coming out to the division along the direct road from Béthune.

The majority of the inhabitants had quitted Neuve Chapelle some time before our advent, but the *curé* and a few others remained. They lived out in the fields or villages to the west during the daytime, returning to sleep in their homes at night, when there was less danger of a German shell dropping into the family circle.

The trenches in this sector ran approximately north and south in the neighbourhood of Fauquissart, Aubers, and lilies.

On the 19th the refilling of the supply waggons of the train from the Mechanical Transport, which had taken place for the last two or three days at Zelobes, was moved to Le Tourêt. On the 20th it was moved still farther forward on to the Estaires-La Bassée road between Pont Logy and the inn at the cross-roads.

In a field opposite the inn a howitzer brigade of artillery was in action, firing over the Bois de Biez.

The companies of the train, after loading in daylight, remained under cover near Pont Logy until darkness had fallen, when they proceeded through Neuve Chapelle and the hamlet of Piètre to the trenches.

The big wide main roads, even on the darkest nights, were easy to follow, but on the twisting narrow country lanes it was very different. These seemed to wind in every direction, leading to nowhere in particular, and in the blackness of a rainy night it was absurdly easy to lose one's way, especially when groping forward to a new line of trenches.

In circumstances such as these one of the train companies got lost on the night of the 20th. As soon as the officer commanding realised the situation he left his company halted in the road and went forward alone to reconnoitre. After proceeding some distance he was suddenly challenged out of the darkness ahead by a voice speaking in German. There was no need to reply. Instantly wheeling his horse, he lay on its neck and galloped for life, pursued by a spatter of bullets. He reached his company in safety, and at once marched back until he arrived at a spot which he recognised. From there he made a fresh cast, and ultimately reached his proper destination in the early hours of the morning.

On the 20th the enemy had brought up strong reinforcements and some heavy artillery. With their guns they pounded our trenches all day and made repeated and furious assaults on our line at night. The first of these attacks was made about sunset, and repeated at intervals throughout the dark hours, at midnight, 2 a.m., and dawn.

In every case the attacks were beaten off by our indomitable infantry with tremendous losses to the enemy.

These assaults were probably made by fresh troops on each occasion, launched in the usual Prussian method of massed formation. Though they were unsuccessful, their constant repetition, aided in the intervals by heavy artillery fire, gradually wore out our men, whom it was impossible to relieve, as there were no other troops available, and who were holding a very extended line.

The situation on the night of the 20th-21st was very serious, the enemy's attacks on our weak line being most determined and sustained.

At Neuve Chapelle the noise of the battle was most disquieting, eliminating all chances of sleep, as the stillness of the night was broken by the fiendish tattoo of rifles and machine-guns and the louder discharges of the artillery firing from the field opposite the inn.

To the staff at Neuve Chapelle the situation was naturally one of supreme anxiety. The Germans were being constantly reinforced with fresh and vigorous troops, while our thin line was being weakened by its losses. Moreover, it was not merely a question of reinforcing our weakly held trenches; it became hourly more imperative to remove our troops altogether in order that they should procure adequate rest. Human nature, however heroic and enduring it may be, has its limitations, and men cannot be kept in trenches subject to constant artillery and infantry attacks for an indefinite period. A time must ultimately arrive when the men are no longer physically capable of offering resistance.

With the dawn of the 21st we could count up our gains and losses. The attacks of the enemy had been repelled in every quarter save one, where the Royal Irish Regiment had been overwhelmed and suffered heavy losses.

A new line of trenches was now sited, upon which our sorely-tried infantry could retire. This second line was dug by civilian labour, four hundred men and boys being obtained from Béthune and the neighbouring villages. The new trenches ran close to the village of Neuve Chapelle, being only about thirty yards from the houses at the northern end and about one hundred yards from my cottage, and were continued in both directions.

These trenches ran through fields of beetroot, the thick leaves of which, without hindering the field of view, effectually concealed the fresh-dug earth, and also the heads of the occupants, thus making them difficult to locate.

They, however, seemed to me to possess one great weakness. If the north end of the village could be captured with a rush the whole line must become untenable, as a few riflemen stationed at the back windows of the houses could shoot straight into the unprotected rear of the trenches at point-blank range.

The weather, which had been cloudy and overcast for some days, now broke, and the autumn rains commenced and continued with wonderful monotony, turning the country into a sea of mud.

In such low-lying ground the difficulty of draining the trenches was immense. After a short time in them one's clothes and hands became saturated with liquid mud which managed to find its way through even to the skin. As for one's boots, a whole ploughed field seemed to cling tenaciously to each sole.

Under these terribly trying conditions, and in face of immensely superior numbers, our heroic infantry remained a very thin but still impenetrable chain of steel, holding back the *Kaisers* hosts from Calais.

Heavy fighting continued all day on the 21st, and during the following night.

During the early hours of the 22nd the enemy made three attempts, at 2.30, 4, and 6 a.m., to break our lines, and were nearly successful, our troops suffering heavily, particularly the South Lancashire Regiment.

The 22nd passed, a trying and anxious day, and it was decided to retire on to our second line. Accordingly about midnight the advance trenches were evacuated and our infantry fell back on to those dug at Neuve Chapelle, the staff retiring to La Couture, the Train waggons to Zelobes.

By daylight, on the 23rd, the new line was established, the retirement having been made in excellent order and without interference from the enemy, from whom the intended move had been successfully kept a secret.

On the 24th the enemy attacked our new line and shelled the trenches and the villages of La Couture and Richebourg-St-Vaast with il-inch howitzers, the explosion of the giant shells from these weapons shaking the earth and rattling the windows for miles round.

The destruction they wrought had to be seen to be realised.

One farm just outside La Couture was a victim to one of these shells, and the force of the explosion left of the whole building only a chimney and a portion of one wall standing. For the rest not one stone lay upon another, and the foundations of the farm buildings were uprooted as if by some giant plough.

We were greatly cheered on this day by hearing news of a success by the First Corps, which had inflicted 6000 casualties on the enemy.

At Zelobes in the course of the day I saw some Indian troops. They were Bengal Lancers, a splendid-looking body of men.

We had heard some time before that the Indian Contingent had landed in France, but this was the first time we had seen any of them, and it heartened us now beyond measure to know that at last the magnificent soldier races of India were arriving to our assistance, and in the nick of time, when our own poor fellows were almost at the last gasp.

On the 25th more troops passed Zelobes on their way north. Some were Indians, followed, curiously enough, by Africans in the French service, Algerian cavalry, tough-looking fighters, but possessing none of the smartness and soldierly bearing of our Indian lancers.

About 11 a.m. a tremendous Prussian attack on our trenches proved partially successful; our line was pierced, but was again restored by a counter-attack.

There is little doubt that the Prussians were now fighting desperately, having heard of the arrival of our reinforcements, and hoping to destroy the thin and sorely-tried British line before these new arrivals could take their place in the battle.

Up to the present all the fresh troops we had seen had gone north, where presumably their presence was needed even more than at Neuve Chapelle.

On the night of the 25th and during the 26th, the enemy continued his violent bombardment and furious attacks on our lines. Wave after wave of men was launched in the assault, but broke and receded each time from that rock-bound line of British soldiers. Though the enemy's columns were swept away, yet they left our people more and more exhausted. Some of the battalions were mere skeletons in numbers.

For brigadiers and their staffs this was indeed an anxious time. One of the brigades was near La Flinque and was fortunate in having for its headquarters a farmhouse which had escaped the rain of German shells. Behind the building was a bombproof shelter, dug at the end of a pit where potatoes or sugar-beet pulp had once been stored. The entrance to the shelter resembled a tunnel or shaft sunk into the earth, and was concealed by straw pulled from a neighbouring rick. In this bombproof the staff took shelter whenever the shelling became severe.

On the night of the 26th the enemy made a supreme effort, and in overwhelming numbers carried the northern end of Neuve Chapelle. As soon as the Prussians secured the village the trenches in front of it became untenable, and our troops were forced to retire with some loss to a hastily-dug line farther back.

It was fortunate that the Germans had no large numbers of fresh troops now available, for if such had been the case it is difficult to see what could have prevented their making a complete breach in our line.

There can be little doubt that during the terrible fighting of the previous week the enemy's losses had been enormous, far in excess of what we ourselves had suffered. Now, in all probability, when a fresh tide of men must have spelt victory for them, that tide was not available. The sacrifices of our heroic infantry had not been in vain. The *Kaiser* had spent the lives of his soldiers with a prodigal hand, and the men who might perhaps have cleared a path to the sea were lying rotting in their thousands in the death zone before our trenches.

Nevertheless, the enemy were actually in possession of a portion of our line; it therefore became necessary to turn them out if we could.

During the afternoon of the 27th reinforcements arrived—the 2nd Cavalry Brigade, 47th Sikhs, 9th Bhopal Infantry, and 20th and 21st Companies of Sappers and Miners.

What a grand-looking lot of men were the 47th—tall, lithe, and soldierly, typical sons of a warrior race.

The 2nd Cavalry Brigade went into Richebourg-St-Vaast and Vieille Chapelle in support, the Indian troops being kept for the assault on Neuve Chapelle, which was planned for the following day.

Artillery was lent by the French and also by the 5th Division, and at 11.30 a.m. on the 28th eighty guns concentrated their fire on Neuve Chapelle. Under that bombardment of shrapnel and high explosive the village disappeared from view under a pall of smoke and debris. It seemed as if nothing could exist in that hail of steel; but shrapnel is of little use against thick walls and well constructed trenches, and at this early stage of the war the value of high-explosive shells from big-calibre guns was perhaps not sufficiently realised.

As soon as the bombardment ceased the 47th dashed forward to the attack, led by their white officers and supported by the 9th Bhopals and the Sappers. No finer sight has been witnessed in the war than the charge of the Sikh soldiers. With splendid *élan* and little loss they entered the village, bayoneting every German they encountered as they emerged from the shelters into which they had crept when the bombardment commenced.

At the end of the street, however, the German machine guns still remained unharmed, and these deadly weapons now swept all approaches with a hurricane of lead. In face of that awful tornado no man could live, and those splendid Indian warriors melted away before the storm of bullets.

The attack was broken, and the survivors dispersed, having lost more than half their white officers and many of their comrades.

Such sadly glorious episodes there will be in every war, but the pity of such sacrifices must force a tear from the eye of even the hardest-hearted.

This severe check at such a time was very depressing, but help was at hand. The Lahore Division had arrived. Its leading battalions, the Seaforth Highlanders and 2nd Gurkhas, were speedily on the scene, and joined the 2nd Cavalry Brigade in the trenches, reinforcing our greatly exhausted Division.

Hourly the situation improved as fresh soldiers arrived, and by nightfall the position was secure.

Our line was indeed bent, but still remained unbroken.

The joy of our men as the Indian troops joined them in the trenches was unbounded. How they shook those dusky fighters by the hand, and almost embraced them in the exuberance of their delight!

The supply of food this night to the Indian troops was a matter of great difficulty. The survivors of the attack on Neuve Chapelle were much scattered, while the other troops were out of touch with their own train, which was newly arrived in the country and working under absolutely novel conditions. Moreover, the caste prejudices, which permit the Indian only to eat certain food prepared by his own kind, crippled our attempt to alleviate the situation.

Late in the evening I was sent to give what assistance I could to the Indian Train officers. I met them at Pont-du-Hem, and informed them of the positions of the various units; then, joining a company of Sappers and Miners, I guided them through Croix Barbée and its shell-torn cottages to Richebourg-St-Vaast, where it was billeted in support.

As we left Pont-du-Hem the German shrapnel was bursting about thirty feet above the road between Rouge Croix and Pont Logy, the vivid flashes of the shells seeming to accentuate the blackness of the night.

On the 29th more Indian troops arrived, and though we lost the 2nd Cavalry Brigade, which returned to its own Division, yet we had now such strong reinforcements that it became possible to withdraw some of our weary men from the trenches, their places being taken by the Lahore Division.

One brigade, the 7th, was accordingly brought out and put into Richebourg-St-Vaast.

No sooner, however, were the tired men settled in their billets enjoying some food and the first rest which they had had for three weeks, than four high-explosive shells fell into the village.

The first alighted just outside Brigade Headquarters, and hardly had the terrific roar of its explosion subsided than three others followed in quick succession. The scared men hurried from their billets like frightened rabbits from a burrow, some taking shelter in the neighbouring fields.

Order was, however, quickly restored, and as these shells seemed to be followed by no others, the men gradually settled back in their billets, though a natural apprehension remained that the enemy might resume at any moment his unwelcome attentions.

Considering the size and destructive powers of these shells, very little damage was done and few casualties resulted.

Some hours later I was sitting at supper with a companion in a house near the canal at Vieille Chapelle, talking to the chaplain of the Gordon Highlanders. With a bandage round his head he was narrating the account of the brief bombardment of Richebourg-St-Vaast, during which he had been wounded by piece of flying debris.

Suddenly a noise like the rapid approach of an express train was heard. Before we had time to do more than glance at one another in amazement a terrific explosion occurred, the ground shook, every window rattled, and many panes of glass were broken.

There was no need to tell us what had happened. I ran outside to see what damage had been done, and found that the shell had exploded in a meadow across the road opposite the house. It was fortunate indeed that it fell on soft ground, as otherwise all the houses round

NEUVE CHAPELLE.

and their occupants must have suffered severely.

A second or two later, as I was turning to go back to the house, I heard the noise of another shell approaching. I looked round for cover. There was the house, which, if hit, would fall on my head; there was the soft, wet, dirty ground at my feet, upon which I might lie and be blown to fragments.

Against large-size high explosive shells one can find safety no-where—even cellars afford no protection.

It is "*kismet*" if one is hit; no man can escape his fate.

Comforting myself with this reflection, I waited. With a reverber-ating roar, accompanied by the noise of falling stones and shattering glass, the shell burst at the farther end of the village.

After some minutes, as no more objectionable Prussian souvenirs arrived, I returned to the house. I found my companion quietly con-tinuing his supper. He too was a fatalist, and considered himself as safe at supper as anywhere else. The chaplain had disappeared; he, I am sure, was quite convinced that the Germans had a particular spite against him, for their shells had followed him from Richebourg-St-Vaast to Vieille Chapelle.

Outside the house an Indian Field Ambulance had been drawn up. They were now restowing their equipment in the vehicles and hook-ing in the horses, hurriedly preparing to move off to a safer locality at Zelobes.

In my heart I sincerely sympathised with them, and only regretted that my duty would not allow me to accompany them.

All Indians, I believe, are fatalists, but these fellows had quite made up their minds to put their beliefs to no unnecessary tests.

I thoroughly approved their wisdom.

To be under rifle or shrapnel fire is unpleasant enough, to be under fire of large-size high explosive howitzer shells is undoubtedly un-nerving even to the bravest. Words fail me to express my admiration of our infantry soldiers who sometimes have to sustain hour after hour the fire of these huge shells, which rend the earth like miniature volcanoes, tearing even the dead from their graves.

On the 31st our division handed over their whole line to the Lahore Division, and the 7th and 9th Brigades, shaking the mud of Neuve Chapelle from their feet, marched off through the rain and slush to pluck fresh laurels in pastures new.

Chapter 10

Ypres

The 9th Brigade marched to Neuve Eglise, where it formed part of a mixed force under General Allenby operating about Messines. The 7th Brigade marched to Merris, where it went into billets for a short rest. The 8th Brigade and all the artillery were left behind at Neuve Chapelle to strengthen the Lahore Division.

Headquarters moved to Meteren, a small town two miles from Bailleul on the Bailleul-Cassel road.

Bailleul and Meteren are about three miles from the Belgian frontier and twelve from Ypres, which lies to the northward. Both towns had suffered from the German occupation. Little or no damage had been done to the buildings, but each place had been subjected to Prussian "frightfulness" in the shape of outrages on the unfortunate inhabitants.

The German Army, as the whole world knows, is under an iron discipline; the terrible crimes, therefore, which have been proved against it in the shape of criminal assaults on women and young girls, and of foul murder of tiny infants and defenceless men, can only have been committed with the deliberate and cold-blooded sanction of its highest officers. They cannot be excused on the plea that excesses are sometimes committed by the best disciplined troops in moments of mad lust and wild excitement.

German officers, moreover, have themselves taken part in these cowardly atrocities; and whatever the result of this titanic war may be, from this time onwards the honour of the German Army, the pledged word of a Prussian and the glory of the German flag have been tarnished unredeemably. For these things, which mean so much in the community of cultured nations, every honest man in future can have nothing but contempt.

On the evening of the 1st November the 7th Brigade was ordered to Locre and temporarily attached to the 5th Division. The route lay through Bailleul, and the streets of this town from nightfall to sunrise were choked with masses of troops, both French and English, pouring through on their way north.

Progress was dreadfully slow, for into the main stream of troops other tributary streams of infantry, guns, and transport from side roads kept converging. Staff, and even general officers, worked heroically to ease the congestion and control the traffic. The difficulty of the work was increased by the pouring rain, the blackness of the night, and the fact that different formations, both French and British, were using the same main thoroughfare. Units of the same brigade got separated by other troops getting in between; to find any one in that river of humanity was an impossible task.

Fortunately all were advancing in the same direction.

At daylight I found the 7th Brigade Headquarters in the grounds of the chateau at Locre, just across the Belgian frontier, the Train company bivouacking in the little park between the rhododendron bushes of the drive and some ornamental water on which a couple of swans were lazily floating.

On the 4th November the 9th Brigade returned to the division, having done excellent work at Messines. That gallant regiment the Lincolns especially distinguished itself

One of the units newly attached to the Brigade was the London Scottish, and I saw this famous regiment now for the first time. Small wonder that this is a splendid corps, considering the material of its rank and file.

From the 4th till the 7th the two brigades enjoyed a short rest at Locre and Bailleul. Early on the 8th they marched off through Locre, La Clytte, and Ypres to Hooge, where they occupied trenches in the woods about a thousand yards east of the *château*.

The road from Locre to Ypres was in a terribly bad condition, the *pavé* was very rough, and was only laid for a width of about twelve feet along the middle. On each side the surface of the road was soft, and this had been churned into a morass by the heavy rain, the feet of thousands of horses, and the wheels of many guns and transport vehicles.

The difficulty of getting motor transport along such a road was immense. It was impossible for two vehicles to pass each other, for the *pavé* was constructed with a high camber, and if a heavy lorry got off the centre of the track the wheels slid down over the edge of the *pavé* into the bog at the side. Here the vehicle might remain for hours till it was pulled out, as the edge of the *pavé* was six inches to two feet higher than the level to which the wheels dropped in the morass.

Sometimes, after having subsided into this slough of despond, a lorry would proceed crabwise with three wheels on the *pavé* and one in the bog until a hard piece of road was reached, from which the recalcitrant wheel could again climb on to the track.

On arrival at La Clytte the Motor Supply Column handed over its load to the Supply Section of the train and returned to railhead, which was Bailleul.

La Clytte is a small 'village containing about two dozen houses and a church. The latter stands on one side of the main road, and was being used by the French as a hospital for their wounded. Some of the lightly wounded men, swathed in bandages, were slowly limping along the street or sitting out on the cottage doorsteps.

Just beside the church, on the edge of the road, were several newly-made graves. As the wounded within the building died they were brought out and buried at the church door, almost in the street. Each grave was marked with a neat but rough little wooden cross, on which was painted the dead man's name and corps. On each little cross, too, was a tiny wreath of flowers.

As we were filling the train waggons a battalion of French infantry came swinging along the road dressed in the time-honoured *képi*, long blue coat, and red trousers; the coat is buttoned back above the knee to give freedom to the limbs. The men on the whole are smaller than ours, but bronzed and hardy, and are wonderful marchers in spite of the heavy kit which each man carries on his back.

Just beyond La Clytte several French batteries were in action, keeping up a rapid fire. Every now and again a dirty grey puff of smoke broke out over their heads and hung in the air for some few minutes before dissolving. This was German shrapnel bursting, apparently with effect, for presently some little hand ambulances or stretchers on low wheels passed me on the way to the hospital, each one occupied by a wounded man. One sufferer who was wheeled by must have been hit in the back, for he was lying on his face, and kept so motionless that I thought he must be dead.

In the afternoon I went into Ypres.

What a beautiful old town this must have been before the Huns had turned their artillery upon it.

Crossing the railway at the southern end of the town, we came to a big open square with flower-gardens in the middle. On one side was the station, in which lay an armoured train with steam up, and a huge gun projected its long muzzle over one of the leading trucks. Opposite the station was, or rather had been, a hotel; now the whole front of the building had been cut away as if by some giant knife, and lay, a great ugly pile of debris, in the square. As the front was gone, one could look into all the rooms. Some of the floors were inclined towards the street, and the furniture had slid out and smashed itself on the pavement below. Other floors seemed perfectly sound, and the beds and furniture were undamaged; even the electric light still hung unharmed from the middle of the ceiling.

It must have been a big shell which could cut the whole front from a hotel.

In the square numberless holes of various sizes showed where other shells had fallen.

The town was still being bombarded; although we had only been there a few moments several shells had fallen into it during that time, and judging by the noise each one must have done considerable damage, though the missiles did not appear to be of large calibre.

As we reached the farther corner of the square a shell struck a telegraph pole a little distance away, and in a moment the wires had collapsed into the street, some of them falling across a car belonging to the Divisional Staff, which was just in front of ours.

Stopping our car, I ran over to see if anybody was hurt. One of the staff officers was cut across the bridge of the nose, otherwise no one seemed any the worse. Fortunately we were proceeding very slowly indeed at the time, owing to the shot-ridden state of the road.

Farther on our progress was blocked by a house which had been shelled and caught fire, and was now lying a smoking, evil-smelling mass of bricks, plaster, and charred wood across our path. This house, like the hotel, must have been hit by a very large-size shell, probably an 11 inch high explosive. The whole house was a ruin, and appeared as if it had been in an earthquake.

We wondered how we were to pass this obstruction. It was no use trying another street, as in all probability we should find it in the same condition.

Putting the engine into low gear and leaving only the driver in each vehicle, the cars were forced over the smoking pile of ruins. It was wonderful how the tyres stood the strain of such an uneven surface, but the obstacle was negotiated in safety.

Presently we came to the famous Cloth Hall, which stands on one side of the Grande Place. This historic old edifice, the foundation-stone of which was laid by Count Baldwin IX. of Flanders in the year 1200, is a perfect work of art, and up to this time had escaped the Huns' artillery.

The ground floor consists of an open hall the length of the building, supported by stone columns. The facade is pierced by two rows of pointed windows and decorated with statues. The whole structure is a delight to the eye, and it is a thousand pities that this historic old masterpiece should later have been ruthlessly destroyed by the Germans for no military advantage whatsoever.

Crossing the canal, we came out to the north-east corner of the town. Here the main road through Ypres, which we had been following, bifurcates. One, the northerly road, continues to Zonnebeke; the other turns to the right, and, passing the cemetery, which it leaves on the left hand, goes out to Hooge, about one and a half miles farther on.

This road, which leads to Menin, is a fine wide thoroughfare with steam-tram lines laid down on the right side, and was at this time a highly dangerous route. It pointed directly to the German position, and could be enfiladed its whole length. It was therefore frequented as little as possible by daylight.

On the way to Hooge we passed several fine houses standing in their own grounds. One was being used as a hospital, and the Union Jack with the Red Cross flag were flying conspicuously from the roof. This had not saved the building from being hit, either intentionally or by accident it was impossible to say—probably the latter.

Presently we arrived at Hooge, a hamlet of a dozen cottages clustering at the gate of a white *château* which stood in a small park on the left side of the road.

In normal times the *château* must have been a delightful place, but now its weather-stained gates, weed-grown drive, and unkempt lawns and flower-gardens gave it a forlorn, neglected appearance. The lawns, both front and back, were pitted with gigantic holes, a large conservatory near the house had every pane of glass shattered, and the stables and coach-house had also suffered badly from the enemy's artillery.

The *château* itself is not a large building, but it is lofty and built of white stone, which renders it very conspicuous in the centre of its park of dark trees. The architecture is ugly, and the building would in normal times be commonplace enough; but it is now famous as the setting of some of the most desperate fighting of the war. French, British, Belgians, and Germans lie dead in thousands in the thick woods round Hooge. The *château* has at various times been in the occupation of all four nations, and when the war is over, from its roof—if it then still stands—one will look out in all directions over one vast graveyard,—the graveyard of brave strong men, the best and most virile of their race, each of whom fought nobly, according to his own ideas, in the defence of his home and dear motherland.

Oh, the pity of such appalling sacrifices! But such have been since the world began, and must continue till the end, while human nature is as it is.

If the whole civilised world will but combine to insist upon bringing the authors of this hideous war to proper and public punishment, then the lives of all the heroes who lie in the woods of Hooge will not have been given in vain, and the first step towards reduction of armaments and cessation of war will have been taken.

The chateau at this time was the headquarters of our division. The rooms on the top floors were used as bedrooms by the staff officers, the ground floor as offices and mess-room. The cellars were occupied by the servants. The rooms were large and lofty but without furniture, and fearfully draughty, every window and glass door having been shattered by the concussion from the shells which had fallen in the grounds. The house had up to date escaped a direct hit, but the shells were continually singing over and around it with a regularity that after a time became monotonous, and failed even to attract notice unless they burst close by.

In the grounds were some French heavy artillery, and the discharges from these weapons, mingled with the bursts of the German shells, made the locality very noisy.

Although I had an office seat in the *château* there was no sleeping accommodation available, for which, I must admit, I was quite thankful. I have no love for shells, nor do I know of any individual, except the hero in a novel, who has.

With another officer I therefore returned to look for a billet in Ypres. The northeast corner, where the road from Hooge joins that from Zonnebeke, seemed a convenient spot; but every house was locked, shuttered, and deserted, nor was there any sign of an inhabitant who could help us to get a night's lodging. My companion and I hammered at door after door with no result, and we finally decided to go in search of the mayor, if such an official still existed. Failing him, we seriously considered breaking into a house.

As we stood discussing the situation I heard a light step approaching. I looked round, and to my utter amazement saw a young, good-looking girl, well but quietly dressed, walking along the pavement towards us. She was obviously a lady, and with her hands in a fur muff she looked as if she was tripping gaily along far removed from war's alarms.

In her present surroundings she seemed strangely out of place, the sole representative of pure sweet womanhood in the midst of the death and destruction wrought by man's handiwork that lay all around.

Being quite satisfied that she was a woman, and not an angel dropped from the clouds, I seized my courage in both hands, and, stopping her, explained the situation in my best French.

Fortunately she could speak English fairly well, and said that the inhabitants of Ypres had, with few exceptions, fled when the bombardment began. Of the houses near she thought that one was still occupied, and we proceeded across to it and hammered on the door.

While we were waiting for the summons to be answered, I asked her where she lived.

"There," she replied, pointing to a redbrick corner house opposite which looked down the Hooge road. "And that was our drawing-room," she continued—and I saw that the whole of the big bay window and a large portion of the room on the first floor had been plucked from the house by some giant hand. The edges of the walls that remained were jagged and untidy-looking, and twenty yards away up the street, opposite the Hooge road, lay a pile of broken bricks and splintered woodwork.

"And do you live there now?" I inquired, my admiration for this girl's courage increasing by leaps and bounds.

"Yes," she answered simply; "my father and I live at the back of the house."

While we were talking, the door we were knocking at still remaining closed and the house within silent, I heard a shell approaching, and guessed by the sound it would fall near us.

Had I been alone I should have sought shelter at once under the lee of the houses across the street, as on the side where we were standing we were fully exposed. To leave that heroic girl, though, was unthinkable, and I lacked the courage to seize her in my arms and dash with her across the street, nor would there have been time.

All this passed through my mind as I heard the dismal wail of the approaching missile. It is remarkable how quickly the brain thinks at such moments.

With a roar the shell burst as it struck the ground in the back garden of a house not a hundred yards away, throwing into the air a fountain of earth and black smoke.

I was watching my fair friend as the explosion occurred. She showed not the slightest sign of fear or excitement, or even interest in the shell; and this attitude was not put on for my benefit, for some moments later, when her father joined her, and the two strolled off to their home together, another shell arrived and burst rather farther away than the preceding one had done, and it was quite evident that both she and her parent had grown so familiar with these messengers of death that they had ceased to take any interest in them.

After some further knocking the door was finally opened, and two old men peered timidly out.

With great reluctance they admitted my companion and myself, after hearing we were searching for a billet.

When thanking my fair friend for her kind help, I tried to express my great admiration for her courage in remaining in Ypres under present conditions, and suggested a removal to some safer locality.

She smiled, and said innocently, "Is there any danger?"

I opened my eyes in surprise at such a question, and pointed mutely to the back garden where the shell had fallen, and to her house with its gaping front.

She shrugged her shoulders. "Oh yes; but is there any other danger?"

What could I say? If the British were driven back from Ypres what dangers might not be found in the oncoming German tide? Had she not heard of Prussian "Rightfulness" or the horrors of other Belgian towns?

But was it for me, a stranger, to tell her these things when her father could do so?

I heard afterwards that she and her father remained in the town throughout the bombardment nursing the British sick and wounded. For our race they had a great regard and admiration.

Farewell, courageous girl. I salute you. May you one day marry a man worthy of you!

After having arranged with the old men of the house for a couple of bedrooms and a room below where my servant could serve our meals, my companion and I returned to Hooge.

By the time we reached the *château* it was dark—so dark that it was difficult to find the way from the gate up to the house, the short drive being fringed on each side by trees and thick shrubs which obscured what little light there was in the heavens.

With the fall of night the cannonading on both sides gradually subsided.

Leaving the *château* later to return to Ypres, I saw halted in the road a long chain of vehicles. These contained supplies of food and ammunition, entrenching tools, sandbags, and other items required by the soldier.

To take these out to him in the trenches was impossible during daylight, but under the friendly cover of night it might be done.

The long line of shadowy men, horses, and carts was just discernible in the obscurity as they stood close under the cottages on the opposite side of the wide road.

No smoking or talking was allowed, and in silence they waited the order to move forward.

Occasionally a dark figure would pass along the line transmitting some order or instruction in a low voice; but there was little need for this, all knew their part in the work that was to be done.

At intervals in the line there showed from under a vehicle a dull red glow. These were the fires burning beneath the travelling field kitchens or "cookers," and if you had crossed the road and stood close to the little two-wheel carts you would have seen the steam and smelt the appetising odour rising from the hot food cooking within.

One could well imagine how acceptable the sight of these vehicles would be to the men in the trenches, who were thus provided with a hot supper at night and hot tea again in the early hours before the "cookers" returned. The dull glow of the fire was difficult to conceal from the enemy when the opposing trenches were close to each other. The Germans, however, used the same kind of "cookers," and there seemed a tacit understanding between the combatants to refrain from shooting at these vehicles.

As I stood at the *château* gates for a moment watching the long phantom column before me, I heard an occasional shell from a German gun wailing dismally far over my head as it flew on in a wide arch, to fall with a distant rumble into Ypres.

Turning to my left, I looked in the direction from which the shell had come. There, in the silence and blackness of the woods, were the

British and German trenches, the occupants listening intently for any sound of movement from the opposite lines.

Away to my right, where the shell had fallen, was the town of Ypres, the streets devoid of light, the houses wrapped in gloom, a plague-stricken city; and in the heavens above it were reflected the red gleams of many conflagrations burning furnace-like below.

Returning to my billet, I found the streets which. I had left silent and deserted in daylight now echoing to the tramp of armed men, the clattering of horses' feet on the *pavé*, the rattle of wheels, and the jingle of harness. More reinforcements and stores were passing through Ypres on their way to the trenches.

I was wakened at daylight on the 9th November by the thunder of a shell bursting some way down the street. The shelling had recommenced, and it was with unpleasant sensations that I lay in bed listening to these iron missiles as they arrived one after another.

Later in the morning I proceeded to Hooge, and incurred the wrath of one of the divisional staff for having left my car for a few moments standing before the *château* steps instead of concealed under the trees in the park.

All day heavy rifle and shell fire proceeded from the trenches in the woods as the Germans launched attack after attack on our lines without success.

On the 10th the administrative portion of the Divisional Headquarters were moved to Poperinghe, going forward daily to the *château* to deliver reports and receive orders and instructions.

The 11th was heralded by a tremendous bombardment of our trenches by every available German gun. High explosive and shrapnel were rained on our men, and under cover of that iron hail a whole division of the Prussian Guard, 15,000 fighting men, the flower of the German Army, was launched upon our lines.

But neither the volcano-like explosions of the giant shells nor the sight of that tidal wave of men could weaken the spirit of our soldiers. Though our ranks were thin, though the 9th Brigade, on whom the brunt of the attack fell, was less than 2000 strong, yet with the tenacity of their native bull-dogs our splendid infantry clung to their positions.

The tidal wave was rent and shattered. Time after time with unfailing courage did the pick of the *Kaiser's* hosts rally and renew their attacks, but in the British soldier they had met their match.

Under the fire of our rifles and the hurricane of shrapnel from the

French 75's the Prussian Guard was destroyed.

The attack continued all day. For some time I stood behind the artillery of our Allies, who had many of their guns in the fields just east of the Ypres Dickebusch road.

The famous *"soixante-quinze"* looks light and shoddy, the harness cheap and uncared for, the horses and men unkempt and ungroomed; but the value of soldiers lies in their work and not in their appearance. The French artillery is the finest in the world; and as I watched these guns pouring death from their muzzles like water from a hose I was held spellbound in admiration.

Shrapnel from the German artillery burst over them, but the dirty grey clouds of smoke above their heads possessed no interest for the French gunners, so intent were they on their work.

In destroying the Prussian Guard our brigades had suffered heavy losses. In the 9th the general and two of his staff were wounded. Among the regimental officers that fell on this day was Colonel McMahon of the Royal Fusiliers. In this gallant soldier the Army lost one of its finest officers. That he would have risen to high rank and fame was certain had he lived, but fate decreed otherwise.

From the 12th to the 17th the Germans continued their bombardment of our trenches, but the defeat of their Guard was a great blow to them.

On the evening of the 12th, at the *château* I saw one of the prisoners being interrogated. He was a clean, smart-looking, intelligent man. On the following day I saw a party of prisoners being marched away. The party was a small one, for very few Prussians had been captured. The *Kaiser's* Guards died—they were too brave to surrender.

At the head of the party marched one of the finest looking men I have ever seen. He dwarfed his companions, standing a head taller than them all. His body, though of huge proportions, was gracefully moulded, and as he walked along, his eyes looking straight to his front, his arms swinging easily from the shoulder, strength and agility were marked in every movement.

He had lost his helmet, and his yellow hair, which had grown long, was blown by the breezes about his massive head; with his short beard, blue eyes, and giant frame he reminded me of a picture of a Viking I had once seen.

On one of these days a staff officer travelling in a car between Hooge and Ypres overtook a wounded soldier limping slowly and painfully along the road.

The man's condition was pitiful, for not only was he wounded and his clothes torn, bloodstained, and muddy, but his attitude was one of supreme dejection and utter weariness.

Stopping the car, the officer took the man in beside him, and heard that he had just come from the trenches, and was now seeking a dressing-station where his wound could be attended to.

"And what is it like there now?" inquired the officer, referring to the condition in the trenches.

"Oh God, sir, it is Hell— just Hell," and the soldier, his nerves overwrought by the pain of his wound, the lack of sleep, and the dreadful sights which he had witnessed, broke down and wept.

What sight is there more harrowing than that of a strong man in tears?

The first dressing-station the car came to was a French one, established in a cottage beside the road midway between Hooge and Ypres.

Here, in the skilful and kindly hands of the surgeons, the officer left his distressed companion. As he turned to leave the little building one of the doctors remarked, "We have another of your men in the next room, perhaps you would like to see him."

"Certainly," replied the staff officer, and, entering the adjoining room, he saw lying on the floor the dead body of a young soldier.

By the letters on the shoulder-straps the youth had belonged to a Territorial regiment which had only just arrived in France.

Poor boy, either a footsore straggler from his regiment or perhaps a messenger on duty bound, he had been walking alone along the Hooge road.

He may have been thinking of his friends at home, or dreaming of honour and glory which he hoped to find in the battlefield ahead.

He had not yet seen a German soldier, and the crack of the first Prussian shell which he heard would be something to write home about.

Suddenly out of the grey sky above there came a German bullet, one of the many stray ones that fell on this road, and in the twinkling of an eye the youthful warrior found himself in that paradise where there are no wars, and where pain and suffering are healed.

On the 17th I paid a visit to my brother in the 6th Division near Armentières.

Procuring a guide from the 18th Brigade Headquarters, we proceeded in the car till we came to a farmhouse, about a mile behind the trenches, where a battery of artillery was in action.

Here we left the car, and continued our way on foot.

The country in this district was somewhat more open than round Ypres, but numerous hedges and lines of trees restricted the view to a few hundred yards.

The road we were following was quite deserted, and though I knew that thousands of men were no distance away, yet no sign of life was visible in any direction.

Soldiers in modern warfare must burrow like moles, or cease to live.

Suddenly without warning we came on to the support trenches, a line of deep, narrow pits running across a ploughed field. The soil in the field was clay, and was churned up by the constant rain and many men's feet into a sea of slime, slippery and treacherous.

Water in puddles lay everywhere, and formed, with the ocean of mud, the leafless trees and hedges, the flat uninteresting deserted countryside, and the dull overcast sky, a panorama depressing in the extreme.

Proceeding along the line of pits, I came at last to one rather larger and more pretentious than the others. Descending by some rough steps to the bottom, I found myself before the mouth of a low cave, and, stooping down, peered in. When my eyes became accustomed to the gloom within I saw an officer lying on a shelf of straw at the far end.

On asking for my brother he at once rose, and with a smile and cheery greeting told me where I should find him.

My brother was commanding a company of which one half was in the fire trenches, the other half in support, he himself being in a little cottage just in rear of the advanced line.

The support trenches had been dug behind a hedge, which, though leafless, gave a certain amount of concealment from view from the German lines, but to reach the cottage I had to cross an open field.

"You 'ad better double over, sir," said my guide, a soldier of the battalion, who was pointing out the way; "their snipers usually 'as a shot across here."

Thanking my guide, I thereupon started at a slow double across the heavy surface of the field, feeling quite sure that the effort was very unnecessary, but that, as the advice was proffered, it would be wise to pay heed to it.

Suddenly a hiss past my ear and the crack of a rifle convinced me that the effort was most necessary, and I considerably accelerated my speed, but before I reached the cottage still another shot whistled past my head.

I felt considerably annoyed with that sniper; after all, I was proceeding on a peaceful mission, and knocking over one individual of no great importance would not hasten the end of the war one iota.

The cottage was a dilapidated little building of two rooms. Half the roof had been blown off by a shell, and one of the rooms was filled with the debris that had fallen. In the only room that afforded any shelter was my brother, lying on a little heap of straw in the corner.

We were delighted to see each other, and, needless to say, had much to talk about. I was glad to see that he had recovered from the wound he had received some three weeks before. He was bright and cheerful, in spite of his mean surroundings.

Despondency in the British Army is rightly held to be a crime; but occasionally to lack cheerfulness under depressing circumstances is but human, and not to be wondered at.

It is rare, however, to find the officer, or that wonderful fellow Thomas Atkins, depressed.

We had tea seated on boxes round a little table, which, with the straw, formed the only articles in that shell-scarred tumbledown shanty.

After tea I climbed a ladder in the next room, and through a shellhole in the wall looked down on our advanced trenches just in front. About three hundred yards beyond were the German lines.

Though many eyes were keeping a watch through loopholes in that line, yet no sign of life could I see.

As I watched, however, I detected a movement at the end of a trench directly facing me, and to my great surprise a German soldier rose from between the roots of a big tree. With something over his shoulder he scrambled down the parapet in front of his own trench, and proceeding a few yards, stopped. I then saw that he was carrying a spade, and he quietly and in full view set to work digging up something in the field. It might have been potatoes, or perhaps beetroots.

Every moment I expected to hear a shot from our lines and see the venturesome enemy drop writhing to the earth. But no! he finished his digging, and, scrambling back the way he came, disappeared from view.

Remembering the sniper who fired at me from over the way, I turned to my brother, who had been watching the soldier through his field-glasses. "Why on earth didn't you knock him over?" I exclaimed wonderingly.

"What was the good?" he replied, "it was only one man."

What better illustration of British and German national character could there be, I thought, than that furnished by this little incident.

The British soldier fights clean; he is a gentleman and a sportsman.

To have taken this German life would have been as easy as snapping the fingers; but it would not have been "playing the game," it would not have been "sporting."

The Prussian, however, has no such qualms; and though his lack of decent feeling did not surprise me, yet I was staggered by the colossal effrontery with which, while refusing to be fettered by any laws or customs of God or man, he yet claimed as his right their strict observance by his enemy.

The German mind is past our understanding. Had our people knocked over that Teuton soldier as he dug his potatoes, a howl of rage at British "treachery" would have risen from the German trenches; yet had the digger been an English soldier they would have shot him without hesitation, and been most surprised if exception had been taken to the deed. It is war!

In almost precisely similar circumstances a British soldier had been shot a few days before. He had not been digging potatoes in a field, but with the water-bottles of a dozen of his comrades over his arm he had crossed the open to fill them when struck down.

As the evening was now drawing on, I had to leave. I did not cross that open field again, for I was shown a longer but safer route behind the cover of some ruined farm buildings.

As I bade my brother farewell he was standing at the door of his dilapidated cottage, smiling, still cheerful. Neither the bullet of the German sniper ensconced three hundred yards away, nor the wrecked buildings around standing in a sea of mud under a grey winter sky, nor the thoughts of battle on the morrow, could depress him.

On returning to Poperinghe, I heard that our division was to be withdrawn from the trenches at Hooge and the French would take over the line.

By the 20th the arrangements for this move had been completed, and on the night of the 20th-21st the remains of our gallant brigades were brought out of the trenches. They reached Westoutre and Locre on the morning of the 21st, where they went into billets.

I was standing by the church at Westoutre as the battalions filed past, and I looked into the faces of these men who had stared so stubbornly at Death in the woods of Hooge.

For a fortnight that grim spectre had been their constant companion. He had slept with them at night and sat beside them at their meals. When the enemy shelled the trenches he had jostled their elbows, and when the Prussian Guard charged he had grinned in their faces, and that dread companionship had now left its shadow in their eyes and had touched the temples of some with grey.

CHAPTER 11

A Visit Home

For the first time since the opening of the campaign it now became possible to give our weary, sore-tried troops a modicum of rest. This relief was obtained partly owing to the exhaustion of the Germans and partly to the fact that a portion of the very extended line which the British Divisions had been holding from Ypres to La Bassée was taken over by two French Corps and the Indian Corps. Our own front was therefore considerably shortened, so much so, that one brigade was sufficient to man the trenches which were opposite Wytschaete, a second brigade was in support near Locre and a third in reserve at Westoutre, the 8th Brigade and Divisional Artillery which had been with the Indian Corps having now rejoined the division.

Headquarters occupied a small *château* on the eastern slopes of Mont Noir, where General Gough had been previously installed.

What a relief it was to be away from the noise and hideous anxiety which we suffered at Hooge. Our losses, though probably only a tithe of the enemy's, were yet very severe, and it was sad to see the gaps amongst one's friends in the infantry battalions.

The task of compiling the casualty lists had now to be undertaken, and as I entered the *château* on the afternoon of the 22nd November I found a staff officer seated at a table engrossed in this mournful duty. As he turned over sheet after sheet of the closely-written lists a deep sigh escaped his lips.

Turning to me he said, "Look at this, and tell me how it makes you feel!"

I bent over the thin tissue pages, and read in them the names of many of Britain's bravest and brightest sons. Some were lying in rows beneath the turf, buried hurriedly but reverently by their sorrowing comrades. Others, I knew, must yet be sleeping where they had fallen, cold and still, in that terrible vale of death between the opposing trenches. Many had been cut off in the flower of youth, the joy of life coursing swiftly through their veins, the love of some sweet woman— wife or mother—burning in their hearts, and the prospect of a bright and joyous future pictured in their minds. Yet they had willingly given up all that man holds dear, even life itself, for their country's sake.

It seemed to me a reproach that I should be alive and well when so many were lying dead, their duty nobly done.

"It makes me feel ashamed to be alive," I replied.

"Yes, indeed, that is how I feel too," said the staff officer as he continued his task.

The torrential rains which had fallen continuously for the last seven weeks now ceased for a space and a hard frost crusted the soaked earth. Pleasant indeed was the feeling of a firm surface beneath one's feet after the terrible ocean of slime in which we had been forced to exist for so long.

On this same afternoon of the 22nd November it was rumoured with bated breath that leave home was being granted, and that the commander-in-chief and one or two other of the most senior officers were actually then in England.

England, Home, and Beauty! It seemed too delightful to think that we might see it all again in a day or two. What great events had rolled over our heads since last we had seen our own dear land, and what a period of time—not three months, but surely three years! At least it seemed so; and what wanderers had we been, what perils and sufferings had we not passed through!

We had landed in France full of pride and confidence in ourselves and in our Allies. We had known the war would be a bloody one; that our enemy was brave, scientific, well-trained, numerous, well-organised, and, above all, fully prepared; yet the knowledge that our cause was righteous had given us strength. Our fight was for the weak against tyranny and oppression; for right as opposed to might; for justice, freedom, and all that makes life dear. We had passed through the black days of the retreat and the heart-lifting recovery to the Marne and the Aisne, we had been through the fire and blood of the terrible struggles for Ypres; yet now, though chastened and sadly reduced in strength, our determination to win was stronger than ever. We had looked into the eyes of our foe and seen him naked and unashamed, brave but pitiless, combining the brain of scientific Europe with the heart of an African savage, joining the skilled handiwork of modern civilisation with the barbarous tortures of a bygone age. We knew now that we had to win. We dare not lose. We were fighting for more than right, for more than the succour of the oppressed, for more even than our own existence—we were fighting to preserve, for the world, its *civilisation*.

On the night of the 22nd two officers from the divisional staff proceeded on leave to England, and on the following day, to my immense delight, I also was granted leave. The period of absence allowed was seven days, and was extended to all branches of the service in equal proportion, to non-commissioned officers as well as officers. Later the privilege was further extended to private soldiers, and none deserved it more. On the afternoon of the 23rd I stood opposite the church at Westoutre and looked round at the weary men in their war-worn khaki uniforms, the patient horses straining at the rumbling guns, the swift speeding despatch riders and the ever busy motor-lorries, while to my ear came the buzz of an aeroplane flying overhead and the hateful boom of the restless cannon. It seemed to me extraordinary that in a few hours' time I should pass from these now familiar scenes of war and see again the chalk cliffs of Dover, the bright green fields of Kent, the life and bustle of dear noisy London, and the quiet peaceful lanes near my own home. What a fascination has England for the sons who leave her shores!

That night those officers of my corps who were also proceeding on leave came to my billet and lay on the farmhouse floor for a few hours' rest. Their sleep, I fear, was not very sound on the cold hard stone. But what did it matter—were we not going to revel for six whole nights in luxurious beds, lying between sheets in soft pyjamas, and have a bath every morning, and sit at a daintily-spread table three times each day!

At 3 a.m. on the 24th we were up in an instant. Outside it was black, and freezing hard. In the stillness of the frosty air the booming of the guns came clearly to the ear. Let us away from the cursed sound, and rest for a week from their grumbling roar.

We were going by motorcar to Bailleul, about four miles away, there to continue the journey by motor-bus to Boulogne. The chauffeur seemed to find it difficult to start his engine and to get the acetylene headlights to burn. It was with growing impatience that we swore at him as the minutes slipped by. At last the engine started, and with sighs of thankfulness we took our seats and sped into the darkness.

At Bailleul we found a line of motor-buses waiting—the same

old buses from the streets of London and the very same drivers and conductors, but men and vehicles alike were now in khaki. Gone were the bright coloured bodies of the General Omnibus Company; gone, too, the flaring advertisements of soap and chocolate; even the glass of the windows was painted khaki of a dark-green hue. Gradually the vehicles filled as officers and N.C.O.'s from various divisions and corps arrived, each with some little trophy or memento of the war. One man had a spiked German helmet, another an Uhlan cap; mauser rifles there were in plenty, with a bayonet or two and an occasional rucksack or piece of shell. Such were the silent stories from some bloody battlefield.

A few of the leave goers had come straight from the trenches, the mud of Flanders still on their clothes. All were delighted to be going home for a spell, but there were no jests nor merriment in this company. The pleasure was taken almost sadly. This holiday meant so much to all: it was too precious, too wonderful to be treated otherwise than seriously. To many it meant seeing those dear faces at home, which often in the last few months they had never expected to see again in life.

At 4.30 a.m. the journey to the coast commenced, the heavy vehicles bumping and swaying over the war-scarred roads. In the dark interior of the vehicle I was in, lit by a single light, I looked round at my companions. All looked tired; a few were dozing, one or two carried on a desultory conversation; but the majority were silent, looking thoughtfully at the roof or straight ahead, thinking of the joy their return would bring to some home in the old country.

"This idea of leave is great," said my right-hand neighbour to his vis-à-vis.

"Yes, indeed, I call it splendid," replied a young officer seated opposite, who had come straight from a battalion in the trenches.

With eyes closed, I leant back in my corner and listened to the scraps of conversation. The retreat, present conditions in the trenches, the recent fighting, and losses sustained by regiments, were the principal topics.

"And has your battalion lost many officers?" inquired a voice.

"I am the only one left in my regiment that has not been killed or wounded," replied the young officer quietly.

I opened my eyes and gazed at the last speaker. He was a young captain, a boy in years, but with the grave, quiet manner of one twice his age. Though still in the bloom of youth, yet perhaps his knowledge of man and the great realities of life was deeper than that possessed by many far older than he.

About 6.30 the dawn broke cold and grey as we passed through Hazebrouck. An hour later we traversed the clean wide streets of St Omer; then, leaving Flanders behind us, we sped on over hill and dale through lovely wooded country to Boulogne, which we reached an hour before noon.

Cramped with the cold, feeling dirty and unwashed, aching for breakfast, we hurried to the *commandant's* office to get our passes, without which no tickets would have been issued to us. The office, however, was a small one, reached through a passage, which was immediately blocked by a mob of officers and N.C.O.'s all dying with impatience to get on board the boat, which was due to leave in half an hour. With provoking coolness and deliberation the Commandant made out each pass, and to an impatient one who pointed out the fleeting time, he replied that another boat left in the afternoon at half-past four. Cries of protest instantly arose on every side. The day of our journey home and the day of return were included in our short week's leave, and to waste half a day in Boulogne was unthinkable when each second was priceless.

Fortunately the steamer was late in starting, so by noon we were all on board, happy and contented. On the way across Channel we spied a drifting mine floating just awash, a hideous danger to any passing ship, whether man-of-war or peaceful trader, belligerent or neutral. Slowing the engines we circled round the mine, while those on board with rifles fired at it as it rose and fell on the waves. Gradually it became perforated with bullet holes, and, admitting the sea, sank lower and lower until finally it disappeared in a little swirling eddy beneath the waters of the Channel.

On reaching Folkestone the sun shone out, and in its bright afternoon light I thought that I had never seen the green fields of Kent look so beautiful as the train sped through them on its way to the metropolis. There were only a few people awaiting our arrival at Victoria, as leave had come as a surprise to all. As the train emptied its human freight on the platform I noticed one tall, dark, pretty young woman bear down upon a staff officer, and, linking her arm in his, lead him away, a very willing smiling prisoner. Happy pair, I thought; may their short week be one of perfect bliss!

I had expected to see some change in England as a result of the war. Certainly I had seen nothing unusual during the train journey, but surely London would be different. The first thing, however, that struck me on emerging from Victoria Station was the large number of young men in plain clothes in the streets. Coming straight from a country where the only civilian male kind to be seen are those who by reason of their extreme youth, or old age, or physical infirmities are obviously unfitted for military service, it was the more noticeable now to see these hale, strong young men proceeding—quite unashamed—about their ordinary business. Many, accompanied by young women, were passing in or out of picture theatres. The driver of my taxi was a seemingly perfectly fit young man, who, moreover, had not even the politeness to say "thank you" when I tipped him eightpence above his fare on alighting at Waterloo.

The porters who handled my one small kit-bag, the ticket collectors on the platform, the drivers and conductors of passing buses, were to me all objects of curiosity and surprise. Why were these fit young men not preparing to defend their homes? Was it that the country did not need their services, or was it that they did not realise that deadly peril which with bloody hands and foam-flecked jaws was even now glaring across the Channel? or were they cowards, concerned only with the safety of their own skins? A moment before I had remembered with infinite pride the glorious courage of our soldiers at Ypres, but now I felt a flush of shame for my countrymen mount to my cheek as I saw the numberless shirkers on every hand. The recruiting posters beseeching the manhood of Britain to join the forces also hurt my sense of pride. Was it really necessary to tell an Englishman at such a time that his king and country needed him? Surely this fact should have been sufficiently patent to all, and while the poster was unnecessary and humiliating for those ready to answer the call, it was merely waste paper to the poltroons who would have been deaf to any appeal.

Every citizen by virtue of his citizenship owes his country a duty. In this crisis that duty is plain. It is quite irrelevant to argue whether the duty should be performed willingly or unwillingly.

I saw England divided into two camps. One composed of those who sought with eagerness to serve the land they loved, the other of those who put duty behind them because it was distasteful. I saw thousands of splendid men being prepared for the strife, while thousands of idlers looked on with indifference. I saw sorrow and loss borne by many with infinite courage, while others sought basely to profit from their country's distress. I saw England like a woman in travail, striving painfully to give birth to that spirit which will lead her to victory. Fortunately this is all over now.

My week's leave flew all too quickly, and on the 1st December I found myself back with my Division, having benefited greatly in mind and body from my short holiday.

There can be no doubt that the granting of leave from the front was a very wise policy. To men undergoing the tremendous mental and physical strain of modern war a periodical rest was a necessity, and, to be thoroughly effective, it required a complete change to new surroundings. By this means the health of many who would otherwise have broken down under the strain was preserved. Sending men home was wise, too, from quite another point of view. The army was largely composed of married men, and a considerable portion of those who were unmarried seized the occasion of this leave to get married. In due time, therefore, these visits home would have their effect on the birth-rate, a matter of great national importance in a war as costly in human life as the present.

Matters on our front now seemed to have reached the same deadlock as on the Aisne. The Germans, exhausted by their tremendous efforts and appalling losses, were now strongly entrenched facing our line, and though they bombarded portions of our trenches at frequent intervals with their heavy artillery, they made no further efforts on a large scale to break our front.

As for ourselves, every attention was now paid to restore the troops to vigour and consequent increased efficiency, and the local resources were utilised to that end. A brewery which was lying idle was converted into a huge bath house. Coal and coke were procured, and hot water was run from cauldrons where beer had been brewed into vats. These vats, scoured and cleaned, now made excellent baths for the soldiers. At the same time a nunnery not far off undertook the washing of the men's clothes, which was greatly needed. As a brigade came from the trenches, where it spent four nights and days, the men in batches were provided with hot baths and a clean change of underclothing, and as each soldier emerged from the bath-house clean and invigorated, he was given hot tea and biscuit.

After four days in reserve, during which the whole brigade had been washed, provided with clean clothes, and enjoyed a rest, it was marched forward to be in support, ready to turn out if required to assist the brigade in the trenches; here, after spending a further four days, it relieved the brigade in the firing line. Thus each brigade in turn served four days in the trenches and eight out. As the billeting accommodation in the surrounding villages was taxed to an excessive extent, wooden huts were built by the engineers in suitable places. By this means every man not actually in the firing line was ensured protection against the weather during the inclement winter months.

Presents of food, tobacco, clothing, and newspapers now began to pour in from friends and regimental societies at home. These gifts were most welcome and greatly appreciated, but as Christmas approached they increased to such an extent as to tax the transport to its fullest carrying capacity. A portion of the church at Westoutre had to be used as a temporary store, where these presents could be kept until the particular regiment or brigade for whom they were intended was brought back into reserve, and could unpack and distribute them.

Christmas Day was spent very quietly, if not sadly. In the afternoon sports were arranged for some of the men. At dinner every officer and soldier in the Division had a piece of plum-pudding issued as part of the ration. In addition, many individuals and some battalions had presents of pudding and other Christmas dainties—something to remind us all of the day which in normal times we spend with so much happiness at home.

It has been related that the English and Prussians fraternised on this day; that the soldiers of both nations came out of their trenches and, concluding an informal truce, exchanged greetings in the zone between the lines. Nothing of the kind happened in the area occupied by our division, but from what I gathered subsequently, it appears that such an incident occurred at one point on the British front. There "the enemy" were Saxons, who have never displayed the same enthusiasm for the war as the Prussians. An incident of this nature, though pretty "copy" for an illustrated paper, can meet with nothing but disapproval from the commander of an army. There can be no truce in war except when it is formally arranged for a specific purpose.

CHAPTER 12

Life Behind the Trenches

Early in the new year I left the 3rd Division, to my great regret, to take up an appointment attached to the Headquarters of one of the armies. These armies were in process of formation. Though in my new sphere I was able to obtain a much wider view of the progress of operations, yet I was no longer brought into that intimate touch with the troops which I previously enjoyed. On the 1st of February I reported myself for my new duties. *En route* I passed an historical old town—a town that had found life for six hundred years a constant struggle for existence. During that strenuous time Dutchmen and Spaniards, Frenchmen, Englishmen, and Germans had in turn battered at her gates and wrangled outside her walls, and now once again the boom of cannon was sounding in her ears, and the old stone-paved streets were echoing to the tramp of soldiers.

But though six hundred years of strife had left the old town grey and hoary, yet she found man still the same. His vices and passions were unchanged: the merchant seeks to fleece the soldier of his hard-earned wage, and the warrior dreams of glory and reward. But though man's heart had not changed, his method of conducting war was now different. The great cathedral had seen men march by clad in leather jerkins, with steel casques upon their heads, and pikes or halberds over their shoulders, and cavaliers in glittering armour with attendant pages in gorgeous costume. In later years it had seen others in flat three-cornered caps, long scarlet coats turned back at the knee, and white many-buttoned gaiters reaching to the thigh, carrying on their shoulders the heavy cumbrous musketoon.

Now, beneath its carved stone tower, marched men in sombre russet dress called khaki—men whose manners and habits were quiet like their dress, and whose demeanour was severe, as befitted a race whose existence was at stake. Under the shadow of this cathedral had clustered sutlers' carts in days gone by, but now motor-lorries with thrumming obedient engines stood in their place, and the cavalier who of old rode by on his white Flemish war-horse now lolls at ease in a swift and powerful motor-car. The commander, too, who of yore controlled his army from a vantage-point in the midst of his soldiers, and despatched his orders by galloping squires, is now installed in an office far from the field of fight, and sends his orders by telephone and telegraph to his wide-flung battle line.

So it was with the general commanding the army to which I was now appointed. With two or three officers of his personal staff he resided in a large, well-furnished house just outside the old town. He lived, I doubt not, in comfort, sat down nightly to a well-served dinner, and slept between sheets in a canopied bed. And indeed it was very necessary he should do so. The commander of a modern army lives a life of continual mental strain; in the hollow of his hand he not only the safety and wellbeing of hundreds of thousands of men, but the destinies of nations. His mistakes will be remembered against him not only by his own generation but by posterity.

Upon the state of his health the fortunes of half the world may depend, and his physical fitness must be ensured if success is to result. He must therefore be well housed, fed, cared for—and more, he must be freed from all minor anxieties and from those worrying but necessary details which make for fighting efficiency in battle, and affect the comfort and health of the soldier in billet or bivouac. These details the commander leaves to his staff, a numerous company of officers who divide their allegiance between two chiefs—one of the "General" or fighting staff, in whose hands lies the fate of the soldier on the battlefield, the other of the "Q" or administrative staff, on whose shoulders rests the responsibility for feeding, clothing, arming, billeting, and maintaining the health of the troops.

This staff, numbering over two score, had their offices in three buildings, and were billeted in the homes of the inhabitants. For their meals they assembled in messes of ten or a dozen, established by agreement with the tenant or owner of various well sized houses. The administrative officers spent their whole day, and often part of the night, in their offices. None of the excitement, and but a shadow of the glory of war, came their way; yet, though out of the limelight, upon their shoulders rested to a large extent the safety and wellbeing of a quarter of a million fellow beings. Among this community of toilers my lot was now cast, and though my new work was more laborious, existence was made more comfortable than in the field. I had a good billet, a room to myself, and nicely served regular meals.

A well furnished dining-room, too, was luxury indeed after half a year of rude and scanty shelter. I found the members of the mess attended the four daily meals with a regularity truly commendable. It was not, however, merely for the sake of eating. These meal hours were too often the only periods of relaxation in the long day. Breakfast was invariably a solemn repast; late working hours night after night, lack of sufficient exercise, and a total abstinence from any form of recreation, resulted in a depressing view of life in general being taken during the early hours.

In war one is thrown into very close communion with one's fellows, and the condition of life with its constant mental and physical strain lays bare in a few days phases of character which might never be disclosed in a lifetime of ordinary companionship. To a student of character there is an infinity of interest in one's fellows, and very often it is not the big but the little things in a man's character that strike one most. My companions were men who had seen much of the world, and at night one might listen to many little anecdotes which brought to the mess-table fleeting glimpses of the four corners of the earth: a mental cinematograph, as it were, in which one saw a ride taken across the stony Syrian desert, or a camel convoy plodding slowly and wearily over the Nubian sands: a picture of Northern China in the grip of an arctic winter, or an Indian frontier post baking in a scorching sun: a snapshot or two of war, the yell and rush of the 21st Lancers through the Dervish ranks at Omdurman, or the grim and desperate struggle between Boer and Briton on Waggon Hill. At other times we were not so serious, and a racy story from Paris, the latest adventure of the German Crown Prince, or the last edition of *La Vie Parisienne*, provided that variety which is the spice of life.

My left-hand neighbour at table was a man who had travelled round the world—a man big in stature, big too in thoughts, generous in impulse, quick to enjoy a joke, ever ready to help a friend, a delightful companion, but sensitive and quick to anger. Though he drank no spirituous liquors, he had a fondness for pouring whisky over his pudding at dinner, to the amusement of the mess, and then complaining at the end of the meal that he felt ill, as he slowly rubbed the region under the buckle of his belt in a meditative manner. His *vis-à-vis* was a small man, one of those people who insisted on looking upon everything connected with the war in the rosiest light, not because he considered that matters were always rosy, but because it sent a cold shiver down his spine to contemplate them otherwise.

One evening all the members of the mess were congregated in the ante-room awaiting the summons to dinner, when a terrific explosion was heard, seemingly at the farther end of the town; doors and windows rattled, and a tremendous hubbub arose in the streets. We hurried out, to find most of the inhabitants gazing up into the starlit sky, where the buzz of an aircraft's propeller could be distinctly heard. Though no one had seen the aircraft, all were sure it was a Zeppelin. While we were discussing the matter a second explosion occurred, but this time farther off, while the noise of the propeller became gradually fainter. Armed parties from the nearest troops were turned out, and a few armoured motor-cars mounted with anti-aircraft guns gave chase to our nocturnal visitor, but with small chance of ever getting within range. The damage done was trifling, and no casualties resulted. We returned to the ante-room, and our conjectures as to whether the aircraft was a Zeppelin or an aeroplane were cut short by the doors being opened and the smart mess corporal making the ever-welcome announcement, "Dinner is ready, gentlemen, please."

Trooping across a small yard we entered the well-lit dining-room. "One thing I like about this mess," volunteered the officer responsible for the supply of remounts to the army, and popularly known as "The Master of the Horse," as he stood at the end of the room prior to taking his seat, "is that the table always looks inviting: the linen is clean and the silver bright. One does not expect these luxuries on active service, even at three *francs* a day," he concluded with a smile, alluding to the cost of the messing.

The table indeed looked inviting: fruit and flowers occupied the position of honour in the middle, flanked on either side by flagons of whisky, syphons of soda, and bottles of sauce and chutney ranged with perfect military precision down the centre. The linen was well starched and spotless, and the glass scintillated in the shaded lamplight.

The conversation during the meal naturally commenced with aircraft and bomb-dropping, and progressed by easy stages to the trenches, into which projectiles of all kinds have an unpleasant habit of falling.

"Well," said one officer, "I am glad I don't have to go into the trenches."

"I think," continued another, "that there should be a special medal granted to every fellow who has served in them."

"Good idea!" exclaimed my *vis-à-vis;* "but a minimum period of time, say a fortnight, must be one of the conditions, or a wound qualification for a shorter period, otherwise one would see every medal-hunter in England dashing out to spend half an hour on a quiet day in the trenches."

"Well, so far as I am concerned," said my teetotal neighbour, pouring a liberal dose of whisky over his chocolate pudding, "they can have all the medals they want. I confess I am no soldier, and an indifferent and unwilling official."

This was my companion's stock phrase, and it invariably brought a smile to the faces of his friends.

"What did you do this afternoon?" inquired the tall Master of the Horse to a smart-looking colonel who had taken part in the charge of the 21st Lancers at Omdurman.

"I went for a walk along the canal bank, was shown over a hospital barge, and had tea with two charming nursing sisters on board."

"Oh! oh!" said the table with much interest; "let us hear all about them."

"Well, one was tall, slim, and pretty," replied the smart colonel with a quiet smile.

"And the other one?" inquired his amused listeners.

"Shorter and rather plain, but very nice, and, I should think, most capable."

"I think I must go and have tea with the pretty one," said my neighbour, pouring more whisky over his pudding.

"Well," declared the Master of the Horse, a cynical man of the world, "the pretty one may be the nicest to take tea with, but I am quite sure which one I would rather be nursed by."

Thus passed our days. Meal-hours, with their attendant conversation, were, as it were, the "*entre-actes*" which, breaking the continuous series of our labours, served to refresh us bodily and mentally.

Our work did not lack interest. A modern army has often been compared to a mighty machine, and the simile is an apt one. A modern army is not only a mighty but a very complicated machine, and the engineers who tend it, and the chief engineer who controls it and makes it obedient to his will, must be very highly skilled artificers. It has often been stated that army officials work in water-tight compartments, concerned only with their own duties. There is some truth in this, for as the military machine requires highly skilled artificers, it naturally follows that these individuals must of necessity be highly specialised. The training on entering the military profession tends to make an officer a Jack-of-all-trades and master of none. As he rises, however, in his profession he must specialise, and in the highest ranks, though he may still have a nodding acquaintance with many trades, he must be a master of one.

This specialisation, though necessary, tends to narrow a man's views: he sees his own work and is concerned with It alone, and this is especially true of the administrative branches. It is the duty of the Staff to co-ordinate, to take as it were the highly skilled products of each water-tight compartment and blend them into an harmonious whole. The "Q" Staff co-ordinates the Supply, Transport, Ordnance, Remount, Medical, and Veterinary services. Similarly the "General" Staff should co-ordinate the work of the highly skilled gunner with the strength of the patient, well-trained infantry, and both with the mobility of the cavalry and the wide-seeing eye of the Air Service. The commander of an army in his turn co-ordinates and blends the strength, skill, and patience of the General Staff with the science and industry of the Admistrative Services.

That the British Force in Flanders is well administered there can be small doubt. It is better fed, clothed, equipped, horsed, and medically attended than the army of any other nation in the field. It certainly has lacked at critical moments a sufficiency of those supplies which a modern army must have to blast its way to success, but the fault for this shortage lies not with the Military Administration, but with the people of Britain, who for years have turned their backs on that slowly rising cloud so plainly visible on the eastern horizon, while they listened to, and applauded, the speeches of cranks and office-seeking politicians.

In addition to being well-administered, the army is also well-trained. It can be said, without fear of contradiction, that the original six Divisions of the British Expeditionary Force were trained as well, if not better, than any other divisions which entered the great arena of war in the summer of 1914. The men of these divisions have now disappeared, either as casualties or by being absorbed into new formations; but the great new armies of our king that are pouring into France are also well-trained, considering the difficulties, especially as regards officers, inherent in raising new levies in war time. For this training a deep debt of gratitude is due to our General Staff. Whether that staff is as capable of handling the enormous masses of men which constitute modern armies with the same skill in battle as their *confrères* in the Prussian and French services, remains to be proved.

As day followed day and the winter gradually fell behind us, the army increased in numbers and fighting efficiency. New divisions arrived from home, the weak recovered vigour, and many arrangements for improving the health and comfort of the troops were made. Baths and laundries almost within gunshot of the trenches were established. The trenches, too, were improved and drained, dug-outs rendered safer and roomier, and fuel and braziers furnished for cooking and warming. Communication trenches for bringing up under cover supports, reliefs, and all the soldiers' needs were cut wherever required. All this labour was not only necessary, but it provided the men in and behind the trenches with that occupation and exercise which kept them fit, physically and mentally. The Germans, needless to say, were equally busy.

An extraordinary incident occurred on one occasion. A party of our infantry, taking advantage of a dark cloudy night, came out of their trench to improve the barbed-wire defences in front of their lines. Heavy stakes were driven into the ground; to these the wires were secured as they were stretched row after row along the front of the parapet. The work was proceeding as rapidly and quietly as possible; the enemy were only three hundred yards away and evidently on the alert, for voices could be distinctly heard in their direction. Suddenly the pale moonbeams shone through a rift in the clouds. In their misty light the working party would be plainly visible from the opposing lines, and the men paused, looking apprehensively towards the enemy's trenches. To their great astonishment they beheld a German working party engaged in the same manner as themselves, wiring their own front, and it was their voices that had been previously heard. Both parties now continued their labours unheeding, but fully conscious of each other's presence.

Such occurrences served to break the monotony of life in the trenches, which was one dull struggle against cold and wet. Anti frost-bite grease and whale oil was served out in generous quantities to the troops, and with this they smeared their lower limbs. To keep the water out of the trenches was most difficult; it flowed in as fast as it was pumped out, and even pumping was a difficult matter when the enemy's artillery was active. In the half-frozen slush, which nearly always covered the ankles and sometimes reached to the thighs, our gallant fellows had to exist. Frost-bite took more toll than the German sniper.

Standing at an advanced railway station one day in February, I watched the luxurious motor ambulances glide up, vehicle after vehicle, with their loads of sick and wounded for transference to the sumptuous hospital train waiting alongside the platform. I noticed that in practically every case the patient was suffering from injuries to the head, hands, or feet. The two former were caused by shrapnel or bullet wounds, while the feet were suffering from frost-bite. Rubber boots to the knee, known as "gum boots," were issued in large numbers to men in the trenches, which, though they kept the wearer warm and dry, were not altogether a blessing. Being loose and unsecured to the person, they hampered movement, while in the attack they were a positive danger, for, sticking fast in the deep clay slush, they would be wrenched from the soldier's feet as he charged forward over the heavy ground.

In addition to the cold and wet, frequent shelling and constant sniping, another weapon of destruction now appeared on the scene—the bomb—fired from a trench mortar (the German "*minenwerfer*") or else thrown by a catapult fashioned after the ancient *ballista*; and with the bomb appeared his little brothers, the hand and rifle grenades. The German trench mortars and rifle grenades were undoubtedly superior to our own, but the audacity and courage with which our troops used the hand grenades on innumerable occasions were rarely equalled, and never excelled, by the enemy.

The bomb or grenade when fired travels slowly, with much waggling through the air, in a high arch, and bursts on striking even the softest ground with tremendous violence, throwing a fountain of mud and debris into the air, while its jagged iron fragments fly in all directions with great force. Although its path through the air can be clearly seen, yet it is difficult in a narrow crowded trench to get quickly out of its way, and its destructive powers in a confined space are considerable.

War, like peace, is made up of contrasts; and while we behind the trenches lived in safety and comparative luxury, our purely fighting brethren were in constant danger and could boast of little comfort. On the other hand, our toil was unceasing, while the soldier in his dugout often suffered from positive ennui. His responsibility, too, was limited to the defence of his yard or two of trench, while on our shoulders rested the responsibility for maintaining the army, supplying its every need, preserving its efficiency, increasing its strength, alleviating its suffering.

At last, to the inexpressible relief of all, the winter, with its incessant rain pouring into an ocean of mud, gave place to a dry and sunny
spring. The trees and hedges blossomed into green, and the soaked
earth rose from the waters to life and brightness.

The spring brought not only fresh life to the earth, but new hopes
to us for a successful campaign in the summer.

CHAPTER 13

The Second Neuve Chapelle, and the Second Ypres

As soon as the fine weather was ushered in, operations of an active nature were undertaken at various points along the whole Western Front, and during March, April, and May very severe battles were fought opposite both flanks of the British line. In these battles the fighting was of the most desperate character.

In the southern sector of the British front Neuve Chapelle was the first objective. This village had been in possession of the enemy since October.

The plan of attack was worked out by the Army Staff with great thoroughness and in the most minute detail.

A battle has often been compared to a great game of chess, in which the players are the commanders on each side, and the pieces are battalions, batteries, and divisions. To look at a General Staff map with the positions of the various units shown upon it heightens this impression, and operation orders detailing the movement of troops from one square to another farther on which is the next objective, convey the idea of a skilful player moving his pieces on the chess-board. The enemy's probable dispositions, as progress is made, are taken into consideration in the same manner as the player endeavours to counter a probable move by his opponent in the game.

The attack commenced with a bombardment of the German position at 7.30 a.m. on the 10th March, and as the first shell sang its dirge over the heads of the waiting thousands of men, many eyes glanced upwards, as if to follow the trail of the iron missile speeding through the air. As soon as the range had been accurately secured, a tremendous fire was opened on the village of Neuve Chapelle and the neighbouring trenches occupied by the enemy.

Neuve Chapelle was part of the German line and strongly defended. The inhabitants had long since deserted their homes. During the previous bombardment in October the village had suffered severely: now the artillery fire was more intense, and from a greater number of big-calibre guns. Under this hail of flying metal, the village, the neighbouring trenches, and the whole German position selected for attack were blotted from sight under a pall of smoke and dust. The earth shook and the air was filled with the thunderous roar of the exploding shells. To the watching thousands the sight was a terrible one: amidst the clouds of smoke and dust they could see human bodies with earth and rock, portions of houses, and fragments of trench hurtling through the air. The shell fire was intended not merely to destroy the enemy's entrenchments and their defenders, but also to break up all obstacles, such as wire entanglements and walls, which might check or arrest the forward movement of the attacking troops. There is little doubt that the Germans were taken entirely by surprise by the concentration and severity of the artillery fire to which they were subjected.

As soon as the bombardment ceased the assaulting infantry dashed forward with great *élan*, a living wave of men, against the enemy's emplacements.

In and around Neuve Chapelle the artillery had done its work well. The majority of the defenders had been killed, and were lying buried beneath the debris of the shattered houses.

Wherever the work of the artillery had been complete our troops met with little resistance. Those of the enemy who had not been killed were stunned, deafened, and stupefied by the hideous clamour and awful upheavals of the high explosive shells; a few were even bereft of reason, all were incapable of resistance. The barbed-wire entanglements and all obstructions had been torn up and cut to pieces, offering no further obstacle to our infantry.

In other places the work of the artillery had been ineffective; whether this was due to insufficient ammunition or incomplete concentration of fire, or to one of those mischances of war which no man can foresee, it is impossible to say. As a result, however, the attacking troops were held up by strong barbed-wire entanglements, and in one place by a single brick wall, loopholed and fortified.

Here the enemy, safe in his untouched and strong defences, opened a tremendous rifle and machine-gun fire upon our infantry, struggling painfully to cut their way through the wire which was pegged over the ground like a huge net. Caught in the fatal meshes, our gallant fellows melted away before the withering storm of rifle bullets. In a moment hundreds of casualties strewed the ground.

The struggle continued by day and night during the 11th and 12th. As each position was gained trenches were dug and the new line consolidated. The enemy brought up fresh troops and launched the most desperate counter-attacks against our new line. These were all beaten off with immense loss to the enemy. One such counterattack was made through the Bois de Biez. A solid mass of men debouched from the trees, led by their officers, two of whom were mounted on horseback and headed the charge with drawn swords, as in the battles of a century ago. Such courage compels admiration, but it is madness in the face of modern rifles and machine-guns. A murderous fire met the advancing German infantry, and in a few seconds that column of living men was but a heap of dead or writhing bodies, a sight so appalling as to sicken even the hardened soldiers who had seen eight months of slaughter.

The village of Neuve Chapelle was once again in British possession, though little semblance of a village remained. The one main street was strewn with debris of all kinds and the houses on each side were gaunt and shattered skeletons. Of the church but a fragment of the porch survived, while the houses which once had clustered round it were now a confused mass of wreckage. The cemetery presented a terrible spectacle, even the graves had been plucked open and the dead uprooted. Tombstones, artificial wreaths, the cemetery walls, and the trees within the enclosure, in splintered fragments strewed the ground. A few isolated graves, with cheap little wooden crosses and the big crucifix in the churchyard alone escaped the hurricane. It was nothing short of wonderful that so prominent an object as the great wooden cross, with its representation of the crucifixion, should have been untouched by the storm of shells, when all around had been levelled in a pile of wreckage to the ground.

Around the village the country presented a scene of indescribable desolation, mournful to a degree.

Measured by the standard of this colossal war Neuve Chapelle is but a minor engagement, yet our casualties in the fight were nearly double those sustained by the purely British troops at Waterloo.

In return for the toll of human life two valuable lessons were learned. Firstly, that given sufficient heavy guns and howitzers and an unlimited quantity of high-explosive shells, it is possible to blast one's way through any defended line, however strongly held; and conversely, that to attempt to break through an entrenched position without adequate artillery and ammunition is to invite costly failure. Secondly, that a line protected by good barbed wire entanglements and defended by numerous machineguns in concrete emplacements can be held successfully by a few men.

The wire entanglements and the machineguns in protected shelters can only be destroyed by direct hits with high explosive shells from heavy calibre howitzers. The ammunition must be in unlimited quantities, for it may take a hundred shells before the one direct hit on the machinegun emplacement is recorded.

When the guns have fulfilled their role the infantry can dash forward and occupy the shell-riven position which a living enemy previously held.

In the northern sector the British left was occupying-much the same ground as had been fought for so stubbornly in November, while a French Division continued the line to the north.

The whole Allied front before the town of Ypres formed a very pronounced salient, rather more than a semicircle, with Ypres itself as the centre. The French front was along the northern half of this semicircle, covering the Ypres-Yser canal. On the fringe of the southern portion of the semicircle held by the British was Hill 60 and the little village of Saint Eloi, both in possession of the Germans. Hill 60, dignified by the name hill, is only a slight rise in the ground, sufficiently high, nevertheless, in such flat country, to give the enemy an excellent artillery observation post towards the British lines. Its capture was therefore deemed necessary.

The hill was mined, and on the evening of Saturday, the 17th April, the mine was fired. Two battalions then stormed the position under cover of a tremendous artillery fire, and occupied the hill without much resistance from its dazed defenders. No sooner, however, were our troops in complete possession than a deluge of shells from numerous and powerful German guns was rained on our devoted infantry. Every inch of the surface of the hill was scarred and rent and the trenches blown to fragments. Under that awful hail our men suffered terribly. In spite of their sufferings, however, these splendid soldiers beat off attack after attack. Finally, reduced in numbers, dazed and stupefied by the continuous and terrible artillery fire, they were forced back to the edge of the reverse slope. Two fresh battalions were now flung into the fight. Storming the shot-scarred death-strewn hill, they

NEUVE CHAPELLE.

forced the Germans back once more. Taking advantage of shell holes and scraping what cover they could, these magnificent fellows with their native tenacity clung to the hard-won hill. Though hell was bursting and cracking around them, though the very ground quaked beneath their feet and was flung into the air as if by miniature volcanoes by the explosions of the shells, with only such food and drink as could reach them at night, aching with fatigue and in constant and deadly peril, they beat off wave after wave of hostile infantry launched against them in ceaseless counter attacks. The most desperate efforts of the enemy to win back the lost position proved unavailing, and his dead strewed the slopes in countless numbers.

During the afternoon of the 22nd April, while the fight for Hill 60 was still raging, the Germans launched a most powerful attack on the northern sector of the Ypres salient held by the French Territorial Division. This attack had for its object the seizure of the Ypres-Yser canal, and the driving of a deep wedge between the British troops south of Ypres and the French and Belgians who prolonged the line northward to the sea. The attack also drew off attention and reinforcements from Hill 60, but this was only of secondary importance to the main purpose. The German attack north of Ypres was doubtless conceived and prepared long before the British attack on Hill 60 took place.

In this attack on the French Division a new and terrible death-dealing device was employed in defiance of the Hague Convention. One would have thought that the weapons of destruction already in use were surely complete enough for the taking of poor human life, without any additional terror.

How paltry and ineffectual are the efforts of Peace Societies and Hague Conventions to check the horror or lessen the destructiveness of war! War is horror and destruction carried to extreme by the aid of every agency which the mind of man can devise. The Apostles of Peace rely for the observance of their nice conventions on the honour and decent feeling of peoples, but there always have been, and unfortunately always must be, people to whom honour has no meaning and whose sense of decency is lost in the desire for gain. To such people one argument alone appeals, and that is Force. And if the unrighteous be the stronger in this argument, then of what avail indeed are Hague Conventions?

Now with fiendish ingenuity the Germans let loose the new and perhaps deadliest weapon of war—poison gas—a weapon which deals death not swiftly and painlessly but with lingering agony.

The attack on the French Division was opened with a heavy artillery bombardment of their position, followed by a great yellow cloud of gas, which, with the wind behind it, rolled slowly over the ground into the trenches of our gallant allies. In a moment thousands of men were in the throes of torment and rendered incapable of offering any resistance. Great numbers were soon reduced to a dying condition, while those who were able to move and avoid the gas were forced to abandon the position. After the gas had done its work, the German infantry advanced and occupied the trenches then tenanted by the dead and dying. In addition to the position many guns were lost, including some heavy British howitzers which were in action behind the French lines. Pressing on, the enemy finally reached the canal, crossed it, and occupied the villages of Steenstraate and Lizerne, thereby jeopardising the safety of the British force in the Ypres salient by threatening their rear and driving the point of a wedge between the British and Belgian armies.

The Canadian Division, the new and untried troops of the greatest of British Dominions beyond the seas, were on the immediate right of the French. Mid the dark clouds of gas and the smoke and confusion of battle it was difficult for them to know the situation. Their left flank was dangerously exposed, and there was the prospect of their being cut off and overwhelmed. These glorious children of the Empire nevertheless were undaunted. Throwing back their left flank they checked the oncoming legions of the *Kaiser*, and then in spite of a hurricane of shells counter-attacked the enemy. In one brilliant charge they recaptured the lost guns, but reduced in numbers and overborne by the enemy's artillery they were themselves in turn driven back.

Fresh British troops were now hurried to the scene from other portions of the line; the Lahore Division of the Indian Corps was lent from the 1st Army. As the fresh troops arrived they were thrust into the maelstrom of the conflict. By the 26th April reinforcements of French troops and a British Cavalry Division had also arrived and had been pushed into the fight. Day after day and night after night the German attacks continued—a volume of gas, a hurricane of shells, and wave after wave of men. The desperate struggle for Ypres in November was not more terrible than this, and the loss of human life was appalling. As for the Germans, they lost holocausts of men.

During these days of prolonged agony the battle raged along the front of the whole salient, from Steenstraate in the north, through St Julien to Hill 60 and St Eloi in the south. Time after time the British line was broken by a tornado of shells and an avalanche of men, only to be restored on each occasion by desperate counterattacks. The French most gallantly drove the Germans back beyond the canal and a new allied line was formed to the west of the original line. Over the ground, now strewn thickly with human bodies, the Germans pressed their attacks in the opening days of May, determined at whatever the cost to capture Ypres.

On the 5th May the gallant defenders of Hill 60 were overwhelmed by a cloud of gas, and the Germans following on, trampling over the countless bodies of friends and foes, remained the victors of that storm blasted mound. Among the many heroic souls who died upon this fatal hill was a great friend of mine, Major George Walford of the Suffolk Regiment, then serving as Brigade-Major to the 83rd Brigade. A gallant soldier, a charming friend, in him England lost a young officer of great promise. He was shot through the head in the foremost trench while observing the enemy. What more noble death can there be than to give one's life for one's country?

On the 15th May, the French, with the assistance of a British Cavalry Division, drove the Germans out of Steenstraate with tremendous slaughter, over 2000 of the enemy's dead strewing the ground to the north and east of the village. A new line to the east of Ypres was then formed, which ran through Hooge and the *château* grounds. Of the white *château* itself, but a pile of rubbish now remained.

By the third week in May the fighting, which had been continuous for the past month, gradually subsided, with the exhaustion of the enemy, and Ypres still remained in our hands.

What the struggle for this town has cost in human life it is impossible to say, but Death has reaped a terrible harvest. Not only has the toll of human suffering been intense, but the town and the country for miles around, within the great semicircle of the salient, is blasted as if struck by some awful upheaval of nature. The *château* and the hamlet of Hooge and all the villages in the zone of the battle are utterly destroyed, and remain mere heaps of broken bricks and charred woodwork. In the woods round Hooge hardly a tree is whole, many are uprooted, while the jagged tops and lopped-off branches of thousands appear as if struck by lightning. The ground is littered with the bodies of the slain, and spattered with the yellow stain of high explosive; everywhere the surface is pitted and furrowed as if by some giant plough. Here truly the Devil has been the ploughman and Death the reaper.

Of the historic old town of Ypres scarcely one stone now rests upon another, and as I stood in the Square, where lay the remains of the once famous Cloth Hall, and surveyed the mournful picture of ruin and desolation around, I felt that I should raise my hand to my cap and salute this mutilated corpse of what had once been a noble city. The Prussians had rained high explosive on Ypres till not a house remained whole—the majority were piles of smouldering, evil-smelling rubbish. Poor Ypres! once a city of princes, now a dust-heap! Sodom and Gomorrah, those cities of the Plain, were not more utterly destroyed. Had God's curse fallen too upon this city?

Near the remains of the Cloth Hall lay the ruins of the Cathedral, roofless, its floor strewn with a mass of debris—broken stone, bricks and smashed church furniture, the stone pillars scarred and notched by shell fire.

In all directions the town lay in ruins, and in appearance resembled a locality that had suffered from a severe earthquake or volcanic eruption. Photographs which I remember of the ill-fated town of St Pierre, in the West Indies, after its destruction by the volcano Mount Pelé, in whose shadow it nestled, bore an astonishing similarity to the scene around me. Streets were still distinctly traceable by the huge ash-heaps along each side, but of houses no resemblance remained except portions of outside walls still standing here and there, jagged, broken, like the stumps of teeth in an old man's jaw, an ugly, horrible sight.

I wondered what had become of the inhabitants, many of whom had returned to Ypres in December and January. Did the bodies of helpless women and tiny children lie buried in this deserted ghost of a city? I wondered especially what fate had befallen my little acquaintance of the light step and brave heart who had befriended me the previous November. Her house had probably been one of the first to be reduced to ashes, as it stood at the top of the Menin road. I prayed that she and her father had escaped from the avalanche of shells.

It has been a subject of discussion as to whether Ypres was destroyed in a deliberate spirit of wanton destructiveness or for military necessity. The destruction of the town is so complete, and appears to have been done so systematically, that there is little room to doubt that this historic old town was deliberately destroyed with the callous disregard of the barbarian for ancient monuments or works of art. Unable to capture the old capital of Flanders, the Huns destroyed it in a spirit of vindictiveness.

While the second Battle of Ypres was still in progress, an attack by the First Army was carried out farther south against that portion of the German position which extended from the Bois de Biez to Givenchy.

The bombardment of the enemy's trenches began at 5 a.m. on the 9th of May, and half an hour later the infantry assault was made. Several lines of German trenches and some fortified posts were rushed by our gallant troops, but the enemy's position was found to be stronger than had been anticipated. Though our artillery had done its work well, many of the enemy's machine-guns in their deep and well-protected shelters had managed to survive. These terrible weapons, advantageously posted and most skilfully handled, took heavy toll of the attacking troops, and in some cases rendered it impossible to hold the trenches which had been captured.

The battle continued during the 9th, 10th, and subsequent days. On the 19th the Highland Division and the Canadians who had achieved such glory at Ypres were flung into the fight and a further advance was won. By day and night the Germans made the most violent counter-attacks on our new line. Though these were beaten off in every case by our intrepid infantry, our further advance was checked, and the enemy was given time to bring up reinforcements. About the third week in May this series of engagements, which had taken place on a width of front stretching from Richebourg-l'Avoué to Givenchy, ceased as the result of the exhaustion of both sides.

While these severe battles were in progress, we who sat behind at headquarters, out of the danger as well as out of the wild excitement and turmoil of the struggle, could only work on and wait in suspense for news. We could hear the guns, and knew that in the seething cauldron of the fight ahead tens of thousands of brave men were struggling for mastery. We were fighting a foe as courageous as any in Europe, and better organised and more skilfully led than any troops in the world. To succeed against such adversaries demanded prodigies of valour and endurance. For one act recorded that wins the coveted V.C. we knew that countless others, perhaps more gallant still, would remain unrecorded, the witnesses and the heroes themselves lying still and silent on the blood-soaked fields of Flanders. Flanders! battle-ground of centuries, cockpit of Europe, how rich are the crops raised annually from your soil—and rich indeed they ought to be, for have not your fields been watered with the blood of millions of brave men?

CATHEDRAL AT YPRES.

CHAPTER 14

"Ici Il y a Danger de Mort"

"Ici il y a danger de mort." These words with their sinister meaning arrested me in my stride. They were painted on a board nailed to a post which was erected beside the road. It might have been one of those notices one sees at home on the edge of a field, "Trespassers will be prosecuted." After having been put up, the notice had been left untended and neglected, the post was leaning over to one side, and the board, mud-splashed and weather-worn, drooped one corner to the earth as if tired of its mournful duty.

I had some letters and parcels for my brother who was in the trenches, and the medical officer of the regiment, who had been playing the pianola when I entered the house, offered himself as my guide. Although it was midsummer, and the weather fine, moisture was dripping from the clay walls, and beneath the wooden flooring water had collected in puddles. I could well imagine the horrors of this *via dolorosa* in cold and wet November weather: a choice indeed between two dread evils— either to walk on the slimy ground above and chance the bullet of the sniper, or to wend one's weary way, perhaps waist-deep in icy water, along this narrow gulley.

Presently we came to a place where other trenches broke at right angles into the main trench. These subsidiary channels led to various portions of the fire trenches. Taking the second of these turnings to the right we emerged at last into the front line. Here I stopped a moment to look about me. To my right and left, as far as I could see, was a narrow tortuous excavation twisting over the surface of the earth with no apparent method. This narrow winding channel much resembled the one I had just come along. The excavated earth, however, was not thrown out into a heap on both sides, but on to that side only which faced the German line. Countless sandbags, filled with earth, moreo-

147

ver, took the place of the wire netting, and at every yard or so was a loophole formed of sandbags.

Soldiers, with their coats open, and divested of their accoutrements, thronged the fire trench; some were smoking and yarning, a few were lying down, others were huddled up with their knees under their chins snatching some sleep. Many of the younger men were eating bread or biscuit spread thickly with jam which they dug out of tins with a clasp-knife. Articles of clothing and equipment lay on the top of the rear wall of the trench; rifles, neatly stacked in wooden racks, rested against the forward face close under the parapet. I noticed the care which had been taken of the rifles. The breach and those parts of the mechanism which required protection from wet and loose particles of earth, were carefully covered with scraps of rag or sacking. A barrel choked with a plug of clay, or a bolt gritted with earth, might mean the sacrifice of many lives, perhaps even the loss of the trench.

The men were extraordinarily cheery in their dull, uncomfortable surroundings, and as they leaned their backs against the forward face of the trench smoking and chatting, it seemed to a casual observer that the war and the enemy, only a few yards away, were matters of little concern to them.

By turning sideways and stepping warily, I managed to squeeze past the men and avoid disturbing the sleepers. My inquiries for "D" Company and its commander were immediately answered by a dozen voices, and with so many friendly guides to point out the way I soon reached my goal. In a slightly wider portion of the trench I met my brother and two or three other officers. After exchanging greetings I was led to a little cave dug out of the rear wall of the trench. This little cave or cubby hole was about five feet high, six feet long, and four feet wide. The floor, sides, and ceiling were all planked, and the roof, upon which was a three-foot thickness of earth, was supported by stout timber props. A short plank bench against the two side-walls served for seats, while a table, taken from a destroyed farm near by, filled almost the whole of the remainder of the interior.

Being invited to enter, I squeezed between the table and one of the benches, crouching low to avoid striking my head against the roof. Once seated, there was space to stretch my legs beneath the table, and I looked round the tiny cabin. There was just room for two without overcrowding, and as my brother occupied the seat facing me, the other two company officers seated themselves on a couple of stools in the trench just outside.

Along the rear wall of the dugout, and running its whole length, was a wooden shelf upon which a heterogeneous collection of articles jostled each other: a teapot, which was now handed out to a soldier to fill with a brew of tea, some tin mugs, boxes of cigarettes, bottles of whisky, tins of sardines, some revolver ammunition, and a few articles of equipment.

The interior of the dug-out was brightened by pictures affixed to the rough walls—illustrations from the *Tatler* and *Sketch* of society beauties and belles of the footlights, the latter smiling as sweetly as ever! These pictures served not only to brighten this little den, but to divert the thoughts to pleasanter subjects than the beastly Boche in his trench 300 yards away.

Presently the filled teapot reappeared. Mugs were handed round, and a cake produced, also milk, sugar, bread, butter, and jam. While enjoying our tea we talked of home, dear old England.

After tea we emerged from the dugout, and I followed my brother along the trench. Every few yards we passed a sentry or sniper watching intently the enemy's lines through a loophole.

Many of these loopholes were formed of sandbags, but a few were constructed of steel plates having a narrow slit cut in the centre, the plates being bullet-proof, and built into the face of the parapet.

Peering through one of these loopholes I surveyed the whole of that no man's land which lay between the opposing trenches, a rough, weed-grown, shell-pocked tract of ground running level with the eye.

In close proximity were our barbed-wire entanglements, miles of wire pegged securely a foot or more above the ground—a terrible net in which to hold the attacker under the close and deadly fire of machineguns and magazine rifles.

Farther on, three hundred yards away, facing us across no-man's-land, lay the German lines. The parapet of their trench was conspicuous by the sandbags of which it was constructed, sandbags which had bleached almost white in the sun and rain.

Passing along our trench I noticed a deep shelf cut into solid mother earth right beneath the parapet. The shelf was long enough for a man to lie in and about three feet high, the earth which formed the roof being held up by stout planks supported at the ends. Similar shelves were dug every twenty or thirty yards. Into these shelves men crawled to sleep at night and to take cover when the trenches were shelled. Presently we arrived at a point in our lines where a little subsidiary trench ran out from the main trench towards the enemy's lines. We followed this trench, which was a rough excavation, full of holes, in which water had collected. After proceeding some distance the trench ended, and we found ourselves in a little *cul-de-sac* 80 to 100 yards in advance of our lines. Being below the surface of the ground we could see nothing without^ the help of a periscope, but with this useful little instrument we obtained a nearer-view of the enemy's trenches and a vista down the long glade separating the opposing lines.

While we were there the enemy suddenly opened a mild bombardment of our trenches with a few heavy calibre guns. There seemed no particular reason for it, but perhaps it was the hour of the evening "Hymn of Hate"!

It was quite like old times at Ypres to listen to the shells singing their mournful dirge far over my head, to fall about 100 yards behind our lines, where they burst, throwing great fountains of red earth into the air. The soldiers have a name for each different kind of shell. The heavy high explosives with which we were now being "strafed" are called "crumps," from the deep base *"cr-r-r—ump"* of their roar on bursting.

The splinters of these shells fly great distances, and my brother hurried back to see that his company were keeping well under cover. Mr Thomas Atkins is notoriously careless, and familiarity even with "crumps" breeds contempt after a time.

On getting back to the lines we found that precautions had already been taken to keep every one under cover. All, except the sentries and a few snipers, who kept up a desultory exchange of shots with the enemy's sharpshooters, were seated, smoking and chatting, on the floor of the trench.

A few yards behind the fire trenches hollows had been dug in places for cooking and other domestic purposes. One of the men who had been tending a coke fire in one of these hollows now approached an officer, and indicating his left forearm said, in a very offended manner, "A piece of that last shell 'it me 'ere, sir; it fair numbed my harm." He made his complaint in such a deeply injured tone of voice that I fully expected him to add, "and I didn't do nuthink to 'im, sir!"

This soldier was probably expecting a severe reprimand for being outside the trenches, and thought, no doubt, to enlist a little sympathy beforehand.

However, he was told curtly to get under cover and stay there.

It was fortunate that the piece of shell which struck him was a very tiny fragment, and had flown some distance, otherwise his arm would have been much more than "numbed."

The force behind even the smallest fragments of high-explosive shells is remarkable.

An officer, on one occasion, was seated in a well-protected dug-out when a high explosive burst a few yards away. One fragment of the shell passed through the roof of the dug out, formed of three feet of solid earth and a half-inch planking; it then cut through several thicknesses of cloth, for the officer was wearing a greatcoat with a turned-back double cuff, and finally wounded him on the wrist, a severe blow. The piece of shell which performed this feat was scarcely bigger than a sixpence, though somewhat heavier.

As the evening was now drawing on I bade farewell to my friends and returned to the inglorious comfort and safety of Headquarters.

CHAPTER 15

The Devil's Fireworks at Hooge

An account by the author's brother concerning the action on
the 9th August 1915 and following days.

The regiment is holding a line of trenches out in the dread salient of Ypres. We are on the extreme flank of our division, and on our immediate right is one of the divisions of that great new army which has been raised through the influence of one man's personality and the magic of a name.

We have been in these trenches just a week, and matters have been very quiet during that time, except for an occasional "strafe" from the enemy's artillery.

Suddenly one morning, in the dark hour before the dawn, a great burst of rifle fire breaks out on our right, and as we all turn out and stand to arms we see a strange and brilliant glow of light in that sector of the line occupied by the New Army Division.

While we are speculating as to the meaning of this phenomenon, we hear that the new division has lost five or six hundred yards of trench in a most important part of the salient. It has been attacked by the enemy, using flame projectors pouring liquid fire into the trenches.

Staggered by this fresh manifestation of German *"kultur"* the division gives ground, and fails to recover the trenches it has lost in spite of several brilliant and costly counterattacks.

For several nights succeeding this unhappy episode both sides get bad attacks of "nerves,"—the Germans evidently expecting a counterattack during the hours of darkness with a view to recovering the lost trenches, and our side expecting a repetition of the late attack, the Boches being aided by the fires of their friends from the nether regions.

These attacks of "nerves," or "wind up" as Thomas Atkins would call them, are distracting, as they keep us in the adjoining trenches on the *qui vive* and put away all chances of sleep.

They are all the same. First one hears a single rifle shot crack in the darkness: this is followed by another and yet another, until the single shots swell quickly into a ripple of fire which in its turn grows speedily into a continuous roar. Tens of thousands of rifles on both sides empty their magazines into the night, and the opposing trenches are distinctly outlined by the flickering flame of light running along their front.

Maxims with their rapid and vicious *rat-tat-tat*, and guns and howitzers of all descriptions from behind the trenches, join in the hideous clamour.

The most brilliant display that Brock ever gave at the Crystal Palace is not more awe-inspiring and wonderful than the Devil's fireworks which are now turning night into day.

Dazzling star-shells light up for a few brief seconds the whole ground between the opposing lines, a valley of death, strewn with human forms, thick as the leaves in autumn.

In the blackness that succeeds the light of the star-shells, the blinding flashes of thousands of bursting shrapnel seem to stab the darkness like continuous lightning, while cascades of leaden bullets and fragments of steel-casing fly in all directions. Crumps, too, join in the fray, shaking the whole earth with their ponderous explosions.

It seems impossible for any poor creature of flesh and bone to exist in this Niagara of falling metal. Many indeed are blown to fragments, and many who live are quaking with fear.

The uproar dies down after a time almost as quickly as it commenced, and the rest of the night may pass in comparative calm, or these bursts of fire may continue at intervals through the dark hours, as some imaginative or nerve-shaken sentry sees in a shell-riven tree-stump the form of an enemy creeping upon him.

During these "strafes" thousands of rounds of gun ammunition and millions of rounds of small-arm ammunition are fired by both sides, and the measure of loss suffered by friend or foe depends to a considerable extent on the degree of good cover available in the trenches.

If every bullet or shell fired in this war had found a billet in some soldier's body, the united armies of Europe would have long since ceased to exist.

After a few more days in our trenches we get orders at the beginning of August to hand over our line to a division which has come up from the south.

This relief has taken place much sooner than has been customary of late. As a rule each division gets a definite and regular period in the trenches, and then goes back to rest. This premature relief, therefore, gives us all much food for thought and speculation as to our future movements.

We tramp back to a village, where we go into billets. Here we have plenty of time to think, and we wonder whether we are going south to join a new army recently formed, or whether we are about to be used to retake the lost trenches at Hooge.

In a day or two we hear that the latter surmise is correct. Two brigades, including our own, are to make the attack, and a third brigade is held in reserve.

We know now what is in store for us. Hell—bloody and awful. However, we are soldiers. Our duty lies in that hell. There is no more to be said.

The exact date of the operation is kept a secret, locked in the breasts of the staff. Each night we have a little farewell dinner, not knowing but that it may be our last. We also get all the sleep we can, for we know we shall get little enough when the guns begin to boom.

On a Sunday night we march back to Ypres, or "Wipers" as the soldiers call it, one time a city, now a gigantic rubbish-heap.

Two battalions of the brigade are going to carry out the actual assault, and the duty assigned to my regiment is to consolidate the line when it is captured. We know that this portends a heavy dose of "crumps" as our share of the enemy's attentions.

There is no sleep for us this night as we march to take up our allotted positions.

About half an hour before the dawn our guns commence to plaster the German trenches with every manner of shell. The ground shakes and the atmosphere is filled with the deep roar of the explosions, while the whine of the shells through the air is like the continuous howl of a winter's gale.

After thirty minutes or so the guns "lift," and spray the whole ground behind the German trenches, so as to prevent any reinforcements from reaching those who may still be alive in the battered trenches.

This is the moment for our two assaulting battalions to dash forward. Scrambling out of their own trenches, they rush the enemy's line with splendid *élan*.

The Boches, much shaken by the bombardment, greatly depleted in numbers, and their trenches filled with dead, have little fight left in them. The two battalions capture the first and second lines with ease, bayoneting every German who resists in the trenches and in the great mine crater in the chateau grounds, where many of them have taken refuge.

Numbers of the enemy are skulking in their shell proof dug outs. Into these shelters our men fling bombs with a cheery cry of "Here's a souvenir for you!" as they run along the trenches. The bombs bursting in these confined and crowded spaces do terrible execution.

About two in the afternoon the German guns pour a hail of shells on to the recently won position and on the ramparts where my regiment is in support. Presently we hear that the troops who now occupy the captured trenches are having a very bad time from the German howitzers which are "crumping" them out of the positions they so gallantly captured.

In spite of these fearsome shells, whose explosions tear the earth into great craters, the troops still hang on to their hard-won ground with true British tenacity. They have secured not only the original 500 yards of trench which had been lost the previous week, but a farther 700 yards as well. Their losses, however, are terribly severe.

In the evening our regiment receives orders to move up and consolidate the captured position.

We march out from Ypres just as darkness is falling.

As we leave the ramparts behind us we see a wonderful sight. From all points in the salient great flashes of fire from the numberless German guns continuously light the sky, while the booming of the artillery and the whistle of the shells are incessant.

It is all terribly grand, but I feel very shaky. In the darkness and pandemonium ahead is hell—hell made by man, where the great guns are making sport of human bodies, tearing them limb from limb, as a naughty child pulls to pieces a doll of which it has tired.

There is little time, fortunately, for morbid thoughts, as the officers are busy keeping their men together and preventing them losing their direction.

It is a difficult matter to control a company 200 strong and to avoid straggling when advancing on a pitch black night over strange country, especially when, as in this case, the difficulties are increased by the blinding flashes of bursting shells and by the noise and turmoil of the fight.

Presently we reach the line selected by our commander, and at once begin to consolidate the position that has been won.

We are on the fringe of the hurricane. Many shells fall around us, but the great majority are crashing into the earth just in front. To advance farther would be merely to share the fate of the two battalions whom we are relieving without obtaining any commensurate advantage.

Undoubtedly the excellent judgment and soldierly skill of our colonel saved many lives on this occasion; at the same time he held complete command of the captured position, which lay under the muzzles of our rifles.

As the day breaks the gun and musketry fire dies down, and a thick mist, so common in Flanders, settles over the ground.

Orders are now received for small parties to go out and endeavour to bring in some of the many wounded lying in our front. I am fortunate in getting in a wounded officer who has been lying out for twenty-four hours with both legs shattered, and without a drop of water to drink. The look of gratitude which he gives us from his pain racked face brings tears to my eyes.

Suddenly the mist rises, and the parties have to leave their errand of mercy and hurry back to the cover of their hastily-dug trenches.

Unfortunately I have tarried rather longer than the rest, and am caught by a burst of German gun fire. The enemy evidently suspects that we have a party in the wood.

For what seems an infinity of time, but is probably only about ten minutes, a deluge of projectiles rain among the shattered tree-stumps. I take refuge in a wretchedly small shell hole and hug the earth close. Never has my body appeared so evident, and never have I desired so strongly to shrink into invisibility. Every sort and kind of shell seems bent on seeking me out. They come shrieking through the air like demons possessed, and strike the ground all round, shaking the earth with their explosions, and covering me with stones and mud. "*Cr-r-r—ump,*" "*woof-woof,*" "*whiz-bang.*" Each devil from hell seems to have his own fiendish song.

Suddenly the fire ceases. Jumping to my feet, I run as if Satan himself with the sharpest bayonet was at my heels, and reach the trenches in safety. I am shaken in mind and body, bruised by the flying stones, and covered in dust, but alive and sound, and thankful indeed to be so.

During this "strafe "the commander of B Company, among others, has been hit, and I have to take over his command. This company is in the worst part of the battalion line, its trenches running through a portion of the wood. We get little rest, as the Germans shell us day and night. I have had no sleep for two days, and am feeling ill and shaky.

As soon, however, as darkness settles down we set to work and dig more furiously than ever. Cover we must have against the terrible shell fire, and most of the work must be done under the friendly shade of night.

I cannot make up my mind which is the worse—the hours of darkness and toil, or the hours of daylight laying bare the awful sights around. I have never seen so many dead before; they lie thick in the old trenches and in the ground in front. Many of them belong to that new division which lost its trenches ten days ago, and their bodies have been lying out unburied ever since. As for the smells, God! how sick they make me feel.

In the wood there is not a tree that has not been blasted by shell fire. Many have been uprooted. The whole ground gives one the appearance of a rough sea; it has been churned into a mass of storm-tossed, broken waves by countless explosions. Not a square yard appears to have escaped a shell at some time or another. This pock-marked, shell-torn surface is littered with trees, branches, hundreds of dead bodies, and horrible pieces of humanity. Even to one hardened by twelve months of war, it is dreadful to see these awful objects lying spewed around on every side. Yet once these things received a mother's love, and perhaps some wife or tiny children are waiting now for the splendid man who yonder lies a mangled corpse.

In one part of the trenches held by my company the floor of the trench is composed entirely of the dead bodies of Germans. There has been no time to bury them. The trench had to be occupied, and there was no choice except to walk over them. The bodies are now removed and buried.

The top of the trench runs into the famous mine crater in the grounds of the Hooge *château*.

This crater is the result of a mine which the British exploded a few weeks ago under the German position. The appearance of the ground baffles description. Of the *château* itself and the stables two piles of rubbish are all that now remain. The neighbouring trenches have been blotted out of sight, and the ground has been broken up into a jumble of waves by countless shells.

The crater itself is a great, torn, jagged hole forty yards across and thirty feet deep. In this great pit lies a confused mass of dead bodies, British and German.

This is called War, I commented to myself, as I looked into this pit of horrors. But what is it really except wholesale murder, legalised and even glorified by the high-sounding title of War.

Murder by an individual in private life is punishable with death among civilised nations, but how is the great murderer or group of murderers responsible for this appalling slaughter to be brought to justice? What machinery of the law exists to make them atone for their crimes?

None, I reflected sadly, except force,—force, which must remain until the crack of doom the final arbiter in the differences between nations and the overbearing ambitions of their rulers.

How utterly futile are the efforts of humanitarians to render war more humane!

Last night I was detailed for a most unpleasant duty. Under cover of the darkness I had to go out and search for the bodies of five officers who had been killed about ten days ago.

It was a nightmare.

With the strengthening aid of a flask of rum I searched for two hours. I turned over scores of bodies and peered into the white faces of the dead. But it was an impossible task in the darkness over the broken encumbered ground and among the litter of the slain.

After five days at Hooge the line is consolidated and straightened out, and we are relieved by another battalion.

After a further five days we return to billets for six days' rest.

Here we are inspected by our corps commander and thanked for our share in the battle.

Thus closes an eventful week, a week which I am never likely to forget.

* * * * * * * * * * * *

CHAPTER 16

Loos

The last days of September witnessed the greatest Allied success on the Western Front since the Battles of the Marne and Aisne.

Careful, thorough, and methodical preparation had been made for an attack on the German position. For weeks before the date fixed for the battle, the General and Administrative Staffs had toiled all day and far into the night, endeavouring to leave no stone unturned which would ensure victory to our arms.

The lesson of Neuve Chapelle was borne in mind, and in addition to large reinforcements of fresh troops a great number of heavy guns and howitzers were brought out from England. The role assigned to these powerful weapons was to batter into impotency that portion of the enemy's line where the attempt to break through would be made.

The lay mind would probably find it difficult to realise the vast amount of preparatory work which must necessarily be undertaken in these days of modern warfare, before a battle is fought, if success on an appreciable scale is to be expected.

Not only have large numbers of men, horses, and guns to be brought up into the battle zone and placed in their allotted positions at the right time, but vast quantities of stores of every description must be provided to supply their needs. Some of these stores must be consigned regularly and in definite quantities to special railheads. Others have to be taken forward and deposited in selected localities where they are likely to be required on the day of battle. All the arrangements have to be made to meet not one situation alone but a variety of possible contingencies, for nothing is certain and nothing is impossible in war.

Above all, though the work of preparation must be on a very extensive scale, requiring much perfection of detail, no word of the projected adventure must reach the enemy's ears.

A day or two before the great assault, I went forward to an advanced depot which had been formed close behind our trenches. From a slack-heap, nearly the whole field of the coming battle was spread before me. Almost directly in front, about 2000 yards away, rose the queer, pagoda-like twin-towers of Loos. To their left the ground rose in a scarcely perceptible swell, to fall again as gradually to the northward. Here, hardly discernible, were the German trenches. To the right of Loos was Lens, and beyond that town rose the long blue ridge of Notre Dame de Lorette. Behind me some of our heavy artillery was ranging on to the German position, and it was interesting to watch their work. First came the roar of the gun as it was discharged, then the whine of the shell through the still air, growing fainter each second; next the flash of the explosion on the gentle rise ahead, as the shell struck the ground, followed immediately by an enormous volume of red earth and dark smoke flung into the air; lastly, a deep base rumble came down to the ear like the muttering of distant thunder. The enemy, needless to say, were not idle, and were firing in reply one or two very heavy shells, searching' for some cleverly-hidden French batteries. Smaller shells were falling on the plain in front, evidently directed upon some of our lighter guns that were dug into the earth a few hundred yards away to the left.

As our heavy guns reached their allotted positions, each one prepared for its work by preliminary, deliberate, and methodical ranging on to the enemy's trenches. On the 22nd a heavy bombardment from massed guns was opened on the hostile line. This bombardment continued for three days, in bursts of fire lasting for hours without interruption, systematically distributed from both field and heavy guns. From 2 p.m. on Friday 24th to dawn on the 25th, the fire was intense. The roar of the cannonade was like continuous thunder, and could be heard for twenty miles behind the trenches.

This irresistible and terrifying artillery preparation is an absolute necessity before an infantry assault can be delivered in these days of wire-protected trenches and machineguns hidden in concrete shelters.

The effect of such a fire on the morale of troops, and the damage it inflicts on defended works, must be seen to be realised. It demolishes obstacles, blots out trenches, destroys all means of intercommunication, kills men wholesale, hurling them in pieces into the air, while the nerves of everybody in and behind the bombarded area are shattered by the awful sights, the terrifying noise, the clouds of smoke and dust rising like a gigantic pall over the battle line, and the rain of splinters and debris showered in all directions.

It is impossible for officers and men, subjected to such hell, to grasp the situation with any clearness, or to give orders or instructions with any degree of calmness. Those who are not killed or maimed or flying for their lives are stunned, deafened, stupefied, and literally paralysed with fear to such an extent as to be incapable of offering any resistance. Numerous cases are on record of individual soldiers being bereft of their reason as the result of a severe bombardment.

A day or two before the infantry assault it was whispered, with bated breath and within closed doors, that we were going to use gas as a weapon.

Gas! The secret had been well kept.

We were astonished indeed: not at the weapon, but at the fact that we were at last taking off our gloves to fight the Housebreaker of Europe; this Hun who never played the game, who blew poisonous smoke in our face, hit us below the belt, violated women, drowned babies, shot old men, and burned down homes. It was indeed time we gave the beast some of his own poison.

As the guns ceased fire at dawn on the 25th, the gas was let loose. The wind was mild and generally favourable, and as the great clouds of poison vapour were slowly wafted over the ground, our splendid infantry sprang from their trenches and followed in their wake. The men were wearing their gas helmets of padded cloth, having a rubber proboscis for breathing through, and great goggle eyes. Viewed by the enemy through the rolling curtain of gas and smoke, our troops, in this demon like headgear, must have looked fearsome objects as they advanced upon the shattered German trenches with the bayonet.

The great and principal attack was on the village of Loos and that portion of the line in its immediate vicinity to the northward.

In and around Loos our artillery preparation had torn the enemy's wire defences to ribbons, wiped his trenches out of existence, battered his shelters to dust, and killed numbers of his men. Those Germans who survived the tornado of projectiles were in no condition to face the clouds of gas and our intrepid infantry.

By noon it was reported that Loos, Fosse 8, Cité-Ste-Elie, Hulluch, Fosse 14, Hill 70, and part of the Double Grassier were all in our possession, besides a thousand prisoners and several guns, while our magnificent Allies had penetrated the German line on a frontage of 35 kilometres in the Champagne.

The gas which had been successful in the first stages of the battle was naturally dissipated after a time, and its fumes were almost ineffective by the time the attack reached the villages of Hulluch and Haisnes. Here the enemy, who had fled before the noxious vapours, and from the waves of demons with fearsome masks and glistening bayonets who trod on their heels, were rallied by their officers, and heartened by the supports stationed in these defended posts. The troops who had taken Loos now wheeled to their right to protect the British flank against a counter-attack from Lens. Loos itself was garrisoned by a brigade of cavalry.

Every German regiment that was available was now thrown into the fray. The fight raged round Hulluch, Haisnes, and the trenches in their vicinity, the enemy making most desperate counter-attacks.

These forlorn hopes, costly though they were, gave the Prussians time to bring up reinforcements, and the battle progressed with the bitterest intensity during the night of the 25th and the whole of the 26th. Our captures on this day included 2400 men and 9 guns, while the French, who continued their success of the previous day, took 18,000 prisoners with 31 guns in Champagne.

The toll of the German losses over their entire front must have been immense. Their dead and wounded between Loos and the La Bassée Canal were estimated at 12,000.

From the 27th onwards the battle swayed backwards and forwards with varying degrees of intensity, as the enemy launched fresh troops in repeated counter-attacks. These engagements broke up the battle into a series of small local fights, and though the British advance was checked, yet the Prussians never ceased endeavouring to wrest back that portion of their front into which our troops had penetrated.

On the 27th they made two attacks on a large scale, using considerable forces, against Loos and Fosse 8. From the former place they were beaten back with immense loss, but they succeeded in capturing Fosse 8. On the next day the British retook the Fosse, and following up their advantage made further captures of German artillery, bringing the total weapons taken on the field by our troops up to 18 field-guns and 32 maxims.

The French, meanwhile, were continuing their advance in the Champagne, and by the evening of the 29th reported a total haul of 25,000 prisoners and 100 guns.

The enemy had now brought considerable forces into the battle zone, and with these they succeeded on the 3rd October in recapturing a part of the Hohenzollern Redoubt. Five days later they followed up this success by an attack in great strength on that portion of the British line which lay between the Redoubt and the Double Grassier. This attack was heralded by an intense artillery bombardment, following which no less than twenty-five battalions advanced to the assault.

In the splendid British regiments the *Kaiser's* hosts met their match; their line was shattered, and they were driven back, leaving 8000 dead upon the field.

On the 9th, they repeated their attack on the same sector, but met with no better success. On the 13th they attacked the French at Souchez, and here, too, were repulsed with immense loss.

The Prussian attacks and oft-repeated counter-attacks must indeed have cost them dear.

By October 15th the exhaustion of both sides put an end to the struggle. From the 22nd September, for a period of over three weeks, this great battle, or series of battles, had raged along the Western Front. During that time the intensity of the fighting and the exceedingly inclement weather had been a terrible strain upon all the troops engaged.

The Battle of Loos was over. It was an Allied success of some magnitude. The German Front had been penetrated in two places. Thousands of the enemy had been killed or wounded, many thousands more, with a number of field and machine guns, had been captured, while the Prussian prestige for invincibility had received yet another severe blow.

War is made up of chances, mischances, and missed chances. To quote a passage from a captured German document,—

In spite of the most carefully organised preparation, success can never be counted upon with certainty. Many of the greatest victories have been gained by following up an advantage which at first sight appeared to be of secondary importance.

It was but to be expected that so obstinately contested and prolonged an engagement would result in very heavy casualties. The losses of the British were indeed severe, though far less than that sustained by the enemy.

That the Germans displayed the greatest courage in their oft-repeated and desperate counter-attacks cannot be gainsaid, but the military virtues which they possess are tarnished on every occasion by their inhumanity and ruthless savagery.

A British officer who was in Haisnes on the 25th of September saw the British wounded being collected by the enemy when the latter retook the trenches in this portion of the battlefield. They were then placed between two traverses of a trench, and there bombed to death.

Such infamous acts as these render it imperative for the Allies to win this war; imperative for the safety and honour of our homes, imperative for the very future of civilisation.

There is not a single soldier in all the Allied armies who has any doubt as to the ultimate triumph of our arms.

Lin nia ium ses audepsedem ficullego vide escionsimmo cotis.

Publinum re in Etra, uterris ceridetimo vernirmandam peratilius vite nos fue aperum publis, facerio riosus, quo cumus ium ex nosteri tricere, nestra me pubit.

Ego enicaet ad coenic vit confes in trit. Bus es consus, ut orum pectur, qua issen seropul vis, que que ante con senit, C. Teresserio vid condet verio, caequam adeliussine in dem te faci pecondum iu se non Itatus, ela opulabe rnicae maionsi iame clude pera, aut pater in ius ex noculiquod in prarbempl. O ta, nit, con acta que dium iam queres noxim peretortes bonsin supio, ne tusuppl icaesenite mis, Catalesili, que con die non ta viveheb erficulla L. Ut con det iam adem pra peris? itatist eriaes suluterfit L. Igilina retristisque a nostili civiliu et Catimpra? Lum essena, nosulvides C. Satum ia ma, Ti. At crivium.

Opublic audem, que crei tum mortus consum hortum re, quonsto cum dit.

Unu iam fur ium simihici sed audeni termis, con vivid in Etrae adessilis, nondem nos, nonveresid consicae ma, comaios inatis sestine quoneroraris ips, num etodier enihili publibem obulto cone din virit; nostris? Ti. Gul vis, quit; hina, sentint publi, veres co ublis. Gerius ingulut quamquas cone conequa te, serterit? Hil vilicemulic vigit; ina, fur, facest int inatis condit, Catus consum hortera re cupio caes Catiquem, comnium ina, ne te dellerbis auteris confecus, Casterum maximmortus omacessa turei condam neristam orsulab iterniquem num temus ad sedo, utum obus intiendem iam omne novivat publiae intemo et faurbit ina, nosula vatum etium ter ac vis lintiac ienius cluteme fuem. et percesta vescesi libunum utustemodit, ponem senditam nos hoc, pec optiaet? Oventem et? Nihi, ne cone inum ilicips, quondempro, ublii portum host conc intem inimus liur. Simplia inatiam pervisqua num factuam nostis hos iam et? Opimus, con se iam publis, quem reo, consi factus huitam o audam iam nihinaturis, factuam pere cla vo, dum fur, verumed manum, quos aucienirtam aucio corem ex nim tum public